LIVING
THE
LITURGY

EDGAR S. BROWN, JR.

Muhlenberg Press . Philadelphia

To
ELAINE

faithful co-celebrant
of the
living liturgy

NON - CATHOLIC

Second Printing

© 1961 BY MUHLENBERG PRESS

Library of Congress Catalog Card Number 61-10279

Printed in U.S.A.   *UB888*

FOREWORD

This book is designed as a simple guide to the Lutheran liturgy and endeavors to enable the churchgoer to understand and appreciate the form of worship which from very early times has been the Christian's chief act of response to God. Readers who desire to pursue the matter further will find many volumes which unfold in greater detail what is briefly stated in these pages. Unfortunately, the number of reference works which have to do with man's understanding of his part in the liturgy is not great.

Millions of people enter church doors every Lord's day and holy day to worship God. In the hope that in these pages they may come to a richer appreciation of but one part of what St. Paul called their "reasonable service," this little book is commended to the church.

EDGAR S. BROWN, JR.

INTRODUCTION

Above the entrance of a Broadway theater stands the huge cardboard cutout of a young man. Legs spread apart, hands wrapped about a guitar, scraggly locks falling across his forehead, mouth open in song, he is (so the magazines claim) the nation's teen-age idol. When he appears girls go into ecstasy, boys copy his clothes and his hairdo, and his barbers are besieged for locks of his hair.

Madness? What about the seemingly intelligent adults who a few blocks down Broadway beat their hands together wildly and shout joyous praise as a young woman makes her debut at the Metropolitan Opera? What about thousands of hoarse, laughing, crying people who jam into a huge open arena to fill the air with hurrahs for the pitcher who wins the World Series?

Isn't it true that there is in every one of us a desire to recognize greatness to the degree that our actions and our words often seem a bit ridiculous? Sometimes we are so extreme that we appropriate a word that has no business being used this way. The lover tells his sweetheart that he "worships" her. Movie stars, sports figures, and persons prominent on the world scene are "worshiped" by their devotees.

But worship belongs to none of these. Not to the golden-haired queen of the movies, the swinging king of the juke-

1

box, or the slugging hero of the World Series, not to Marx, Lincoln, or Luther, no, not even to the saints or the Virgin Mary. Worship belongs to God, and to him alone.

Why is it that our enthusiasm for these "saints" of the theater, the sports world, and the political arena, may reach greater heights than for the Almighty? Why must we constantly urge people to come to church for worship while they fight madly to "adore" their heroes and heroines?

Lutherans have high regard for the forms of their worship. Their liturgies are carefully built upon the best of the past, thereby demonstrating continuity with the church throughout the ages. In addition, hymns are chosen for their soundness of theology, beauty, and adaptability to the American scene.

But worship, for all of the efforts of scholars, pastors, musicians, and teachers, is frequently listless. Some say that there is no warmth in it, no room for spontaneous enthusiasm. The answer, they say, is to adopt the heartfelt emotional devices of the fervent sectarian groups. The kind of emotionalism they would like to see in our churches may be enlivening for a while, but in time the ardor cools, and soon it is just another form.

On the other hand, there are those who claim that worship must take on more of the trappings and ceremonies of the early church or of the Middle Ages. They argue that the church in its worship must appeal not only to the mind and the heart but to all the senses as well.

If one considers the traditions out of which the worship of the church grew and the psychological factors involved, there would seem to be much to support this argument. But it must never be forgotten that the mere accumulation of forms and ceremonies, without any vital relationship to the evangelical faith by which God unites us with himself, is as shallow and foolish as are the emotional stunts of the Holy Rollers.

Obviously the primary concern isn't with externals. First of all we must give attention to what we say and think in our worship. The form we use must be meaningful. It must be more than words; it must express our hearts and minds accurately, completely, fervently. Only when we have reached this step can we turn our thoughts to externals.

This does not mean that we must throw out all vestments, furnishings, and gestures, and start in the plainness of a Quaker meeting house. Rather we ought to keep on as we have in the past, but give careful thought and investigation to what we do, how we do it, and what is the result.

There are many kinds of forms used in worship in Lutheran churches, but the most important, and the one with which we are concerned here, is that which provides for the observance of Christ's command to "do this in remembrance of me." Seen in its entirety this is the full liturgy based upon the traditional order of the Western church which includes both sermon and the Lord's Supper. Commonly, however, it is the practice in most Lutheran churches of America to use only the first part of this order on ordinary Sundays, reserving the celebration of the sacrament for certain stated times throughout the year. In recent years, it is evident from surveys of parish practice, the sacrament is being celebrated with greater frequency among us.

In the wake of renewed interest in the liturgy it has also become apparent that there is a confusion of terms. Holy Communion, the Lord's Supper, the Service, the Sacrament of the Altar, and in a few isolated instances, Eucharist and even mass, are all terms used to describe the liturgy. Each has historical significance and those who use these terms know what they mean, yet none is completely adequate. "Holy Communion" and "Sacrament of the Altar" are properly descriptive of God's gift in the act of eating and drinking. "The Lord's Supper" is used by scholars to refer specifically to the event in the Upper Room. When we use "the Service" we generally mean the forepart of the liturgy, the traditional *missa catechumenorum*, which omits the giving of the sacrament. "Eucharist," a Greek word meaning "to give thanks," stresses only man's action in the order, while "mass," although used by many European Lutherans today, has connotations of Roman Catholic practice which are unacceptable to evangelical Christianity. To speak of the liturgy is also confusing; technically the term refers only to the order for Holy Communion but popular usage has broadened it to include all orders of worship.

If one term must be chosen to designate the rite we use, let us use the Sacrament of the Altar. This is the term Luther used in *The Small Catechism*. It has significance furthermore in that it stresses the two-way action of our worship. "Sacrament" is a gift and indicates the initiating activity of God who comes to man. When the emphasis is placed upon what God does for man, we are in no danger of perverting the Lord's Supper. Always and uppermost it is God's gift. Altar is a place of sacrifice, and in our liturgy the word "sacrifice" has a twofold meaning. First, the Lord's Supper makes the benefits of Christ's sacrifice on Calvary real and present to us. Furthermore, all our actions in response to God's gift may properly be called sacrifices provided that they are understood not as deserving of God's goodness, but rather expressive of the gratitude we have because of him.

The term "Sacrament of the Altar" also serves to remind us that Lutherans receive the sacrament at the altar from the hands of the minister, not in the pews.

What follows, then, looks hard at the liturgy. The writer has endeavored to dissect the form, giving a brief historical background, explaining the significance of each part for the worshiper, and suggesting how he and the pastor together with the members of the choir may achieve the proper attitude. Where there is honest difference of interpretation and practice, effort has been made to state both sides fairly.

The church has a glorious opportunity. We are on the crest of a wave of popular religious sentiment. It is important that the church take advantage of this.

To be sure, our chief appeal will lie in the kind of life our neighbors see in us as Christians. If they can see in us a faith which surmounts the obstacles of life, which endows us with courage to do God's will no matter what, the church will benefit and mankind be blessed.

Where then shall we Christians be fed with the food that can make us strong in the spirit, and so bear witness in the world? Luther said that he was often not so certain, not so strong outside, but in the midst of the assembly of God's people, strengthened by Word and Sacrament, and buttressed by prayer and devotion, he knew what was right. How necessary then that our worship be the all-important, vital, joyous moment with God which saturates all of life.

LITURGY

Language in the church stands in two worlds. With the modern world the church seeks to make itself understood, but unlike the modern world, which is quick to discard words whose meaning has been dulled, the church continues to rely upon words which for the most part have become exclusively its own. Even among groups which have rejected pre-Reformation tradition and have sought vigorously to speak to their people in their own language, it has been found impossible to divorce language from its footing in the past.

Because the infant church first made its way through a Greek culture, the church spoke Greek, and it was out of this era that the church first adopted the word "liturgy." From two Greek words, *leitos* which means "public" or "the people's," and *ergon* meaning "work," there came two words used in the New Testament: *leitourgein,* "a public work," which came to be used for "service to the state," and *leitourgos,* "a public service." This is the origin of the word "liturgy."

Even in those days the word had two meanings. In Romans 13:6 Paul refers to the rulers of the state as "God's ministers," yet in a more particular sense, the word came to have a specifically Christian usage (Luke 1:23, Acts 13:2, II Cor. 9:12, Phil. 2:17, 30, and Heb. 9:21). In

6

Romans 15:16, Paul describes himself as a "minister" (*leitourgon*) of Jesus Christ. Notice that the term had not yet been relegated solely to acts of ritual worship. The Christian's entire response to God, his "service" or "ministry," whether in the church through rites or outside the church in what we might today call social work, was regarded as his "liturgy." Only after the fifth century does "liturgy" come to be used exclusively for the action of Christians as they assemble for worship in their churches.

Certain other words have fallen into the same pattern. "Worship" and "service" both had broader implications for the Christian, but they too have been narrowed until "worship" as used among us seldom means more than what we do in the church. Yet quite properly all that we do, whether in the prayers and hymns and rites of the church or in actions of kindness and concern to our fellows, when done under the guidance of the Holy Spirit, is our "worship."

Liturgy thus came to mean any form or rite of service used at worship. At a later time the word was so restricted that among some people today it is used only to describe the rite of the Holy Communion. It is in this sense that the word is used here.

Several other words of worship require explanation. "Order" implies a formal pattern of worship. That there might be an understanding among the participants, a definite progression has to be fixed. People need to know what to expect. Worship in the church is a corporate expression and not just the response of individuals. It is important therefore that there be order.

Order must take on a form. It needs to express itself in words. These words in their totality make up the *rite* or *ritual*. The Lutheran Rite, for example, is the formal pattern of worship, from Invocation to Benediction, which one finds in the *Service Book and Hymnal*. It is the collection of words and music, including a provision for silence, which enables the congregation to make its united response to God. In the rite there is ample room for variety in spite of the fixed character of its form. Several alternates are provided and, depending upon the decision of the local congregation, the rite may be either said or sung.

Along with the words and music which are the rite, there are also certain *ceremonial* provisions. Words are not enough, for there has to be movement and action. Worship would be rather dull if people assembled and just sat for the whole time, but even that too is action. We are doing something. The liturgy makes many directions for ceremonial. We stand at the beginning of the service. During the Confession of Sins, minister and people kneel. We sit for the Lesson and the Epistle but stand for the Gospel. These are a few of the ceremonies provided in the *Service Book and Hymnal*. There are others which, while not mentioned in the book, are so much a part of our tradition that we are surprised to find that they are not "official." The customary choir "processional," the lighting of altar candles by the acolytes, the wearing of certain vestments—these are a few of the provisions we make for ceremony. In the Lutheran tradition these are all free. One may take them or leave them, but by mutual consent our church has maintained a tradition which gleans the best from historic liturgical practice.

All these are designed to make the liturgy, the vehicle of our response to God, more meaningful. But where does our liturgy come from?

There are two streams of worship, derived in large part from Jewish sources but influenced to a degree by the practices of non-Christian religions, which form the basis of the liturgy. One represents the teaching worship of the synagogue, and the other is a combination of the temple rites and the fellowship meal of the Jewish home which found expression in the Passover and the Seder. Because of our Lord's actions on the night before his death and particularly because of the unusual words he spoke during that meal, those events have been incorporated into the Christian liturgy.

Thus the liturgy has three parts. The first involves preparation. For a long time this was made privately by people before they came to church, and includes everything from the Invocation to the Introit.

The second portion, actually the first of the two historic divisions, begins with the Introit and concludes with the sermon. Its character, as distinguished from the portion which follows it, suggests a dialogue. It is the teaching part of the liturgy. We speak to God and he speaks to us. In ancient times when worship was restricted to members of the Christian community, catechumens, that is, those who had not yet been admitted into full fellowship in the church, were permitted to attend this part of the service, hence the name *missa catechumenorum* or "mass of the catechumens." This part has sometimes been called the liturgy of the Word. The name is not entirely accurate because the Word is also present in other portions of the liturgy.

What followed was open only to the initiated or baptized. It was a solemn and for a long time secret celebration of the events of the Lord's last meal with his disciples. The catechumens and those under discipline were told to withdraw, the doors were shut, and the liturgy continued with the Offertory, and concluded with the Blessing or Benediction after all had communed. Because of its character, the term *missa fidelium* ("mass of the faithful") was adopted.

To further understand the liturgy we might liken it to the human body. Like the body it has a skeleton. This is the constant part, the basic and unchanging structure, and is known as the Ordinary. Every time the liturgy is celebrated, this part never changes. Other portions, which might be likened to man's outer appearance—what makes him distinctive from his fellows—are the variable or changing sections. Along with the constant, unvarying skeleton of the liturgy, there are those portions which, Sunday after Sunday and holyday after holyday, bring to the liturgy the peculiar emphasis of the day being observed. These are known as the Propers (or *Propria,* a Latin word meaning the same thing) and by the very word indicate that they are "proper" only for that day. These include the Introit, the Collect, the Lesson, the Epistle, the Gradual, the Gospel, and to a lesser extent the Proper Prefaces. The following chart shows the division of the liturgy according to what we have said thus far.

THE LITURGY

According to the Rite of the *Service Book and Hymnal*

The Ordinary	*The Propers*
PREPARATION	
*Hymn	
The Invocation	
The Confession of Sins	
(alternate forms)	
The Absolution	
(alternate forms)	
THE LITURGY OF THE WORD	
	The Introit
The Introit (Gloria Patri)	(Antiphon and Psalm
Kyrie	Verse)
(alternate forms)	
Gloria in Excelsis	

Salutation and Response

The Collect
*The Lesson
The Epistle
The Gradual
(alternate forms)
The Gospel

The Creed
The Hymn
The Sermon
The Votum

THE LITURGY OF THE UPPER ROOM

The Offertory and Offering
The Preparation of the Elements
The Prayer of the Church
Hymn
The Preface

Proper Prefaces

The Sanctus
The Prayer of Thanksgiving
(alternate forms)
The Pax
Agnus Dei
The Communion
*The Nunc Dimittis
The Post-Communion Prayer
The Benedicamus
The Benediction
*Hymn

*(optional)

INVOCATION

"Who is God?" Parents of a small child (not to mention pastors and theologians) know how exasperating that question can be. How does one explain God to a child?

A cartoon showed a little girl kneeling beside her bed in prayer. The mother sat on the edge of the bed and a boy stood at her side. Below was the caption, "I'd better wait, Mom, the line's still busy."

Childish, of course, but what do you mean when you talk about God? If you have come to church on Sunday to be with him, if you expect to get something from him and in turn tell him what you think of him, you ought to have an idea about him. But who is God?

Some people think of God as an old man seated on a rainbow. Many imagine that God's voice, as a recent movie critic put it, is a deep resonant sound like that of a popular television announcer. Others, who have dismissed such notions as childish, suppose him to be a sort of mighty power or spirit at the center of all life. They like the words of Genesis, "the Spirit of God moved upon the face of the waters." You can't picture God, they say, but he created everything out of nothing. He continues to create and sustain life, and (some of them say) he is interested in us.

How can anyone form a picture of what cannot be pictured? Does this mean then that we ought not think about God? Certainly not. But where shall we start?

Because we know best what our senses tell us, we must look about us and then into history. Here, of course, we find Jesus. From the New Testament we learn of his life.

The sermons he preached have a revolutionary flavor we find nowhere else in history. Who ever before suggested that we ought not be anxious about tomorrow? "Huh? I'd never get anything done." Or who ever directed us to turn the other cheek? "I'm not going to let anybody walk over me!"

But, important as his teachings are, there is something greater. That is Jesus himself. Here was One whose ideas were overshadowed by his very being. Some would say that he wasn't a success. After all, to get yourself killed (and as a criminal) before you reach thirty-five doesn't seem a very effective life.

But those who study the records see the great significance of that horrible death. Aided by the precise logic and rich imagery of Paul's letters, they come to see the purpose of the One we call Jesus Christ. By the perfect obedience of One who had come forth from God, and was in a real sense God, yet truly a man, mankind was made right again with God. In this Man, men could see hope for something more permanent than this life.

Jesus said, "I and my Father are one." "Before Abraham was, I am." "No man cometh unto the Father but by me." These thoughts one can appreciate only against the background of the Old Testament.

This Old Testament is the story of a people for whom recognition of the Lord God was their destiny. In their history, their devotion and disobedience, their conquests and defeats, over all stands the figure of the mighty Lord God.

There is something else one can't escape as he reads the

story of Israel. Like a river which suddenly bubbles out of the ground, then disappears only to resurge again, there are in the Old Testament the precious gems of prophecy telling that one day God will send to the earth a Savior, a Messiah.

Since Christ wears the crown of the Messiah, and yet is the Suffering Servant who comes to save Israel, his light brings the God of Jacob into brilliance. It is from Jesus that we have a new understanding of the Lord. This is not an angry old man, but a loving Father, who, while bound to his unchangeable law, shows men his great concern for them. How better to realize this than to remember that, as Christ taught us, when we pray we say, "Our Father. . . ."

So the picture is in sharper focus. We see Christ. He was once on the earth. So we depict him in crucifixes and statues and pictures, and it is not a violation of the first commandment so long as we do not convey to the image what belongs to God.

From our Lord's description of the powerful Creator, we know him as our heavenly Father. We cannot have a picture of his features, but we do know his nature. That is one reason it is not wrong to encourage little children to visualize him in the way they do.

But even this is only a partial picture. All this didn't end on the cross, or in the garden, or even in the mount of the ascension. Christ didn't come to us simply to give us an example, then wave farewell, hoping we would make out all right.

He knew that even with his perfect life before us, we are still subject to all sorts of desires, most of them quite opposed to what he called his Father's will. He knew that we would need help, and so he promised us One whom he called the Comforter. He would come not to baby us but to give us strength, courage, comfort, grace. The Spirit moves us to do what is right. He whispers "church" when our minds think "golf." He cautions "love" when our hearts shout "hate." He counsels "faith" when we feel "doubt."

This is what we mean by God. God is our Maker, who creates life and continues to sustain it. God is our Savior, who once lived here with us, achieved for us the hope of being with him forever, and continues to plead for us in spite of our selfishness and shortcomings. God is the Holy Spirit, who provides us with all we need to make our pilgrimage through this life and so pass to the one beyond. All this is God, and yet God is—more than we can imagine, more than we can ever know until we stand before him.

So we begin our act of worship in the church "In the Name of the Father, and of the Son, and of the Holy Ghost." This is truly an invoking of God, not a call to worship. As we hear the glorious words we are reminded of our baptism, when by these words we were made members of Christ . . . of our marriage when by the same words we and our spouse were united. It is the church's great formula of blessing. It is the door through which we pass into the presence of the Almighty.

AMEN

A couple of years ago a prominent television comedian used to do a funny sketch. It was a take-off on the way we live, and particularly the things we say. The skit held modern man up to himself for a good hearty laugh.

The comic would be met by another character who would state some obvious fact, like "More cars on the highway" or "Prices are certainly going up." A knowing look would come over our hero's face. Smugly gazing upon the speaker, he would remark, "You can say that again."

How often have you said the same words? The thought that prompted them was so obvious that the words may have lost their freshness. Perhaps you could have even guessed they were coming. Still you fell into the pattern, and to add emphasis you replied, "You can say that again."

Sometimes we wish we could have something repeated for us, but not because it is obvious and we knew it all along. We want to hear it over again because we like it. The thought was dressed in rich, descriptive imagery. We agreed with what we heard, but especially we liked the way it was put. So strongly did it imprint itself upon our minds that it bore repetition. It's good, we agree. "Say it again."

This happens in some churches. A chaplain was conducting a Lenten service in a housing project. The service

16

was just about to begin when he noticed an elderly couple enter the hall that served as the chapel. Sliding into the last row of the noisy metal folding chairs, they knelt, made the sign of the cross and sat down. They're confused, he thought. Probably some Roman Catholics who think it's time for mass.

As often as he could, he watched them. They stayed, found their way along in the service, and seemed quite at home. By the time for the sermon, he had forgotten them and was preaching earnestly when suddenly he heard a voice raised. It was just a word or two, not loud but it could be heard.

The chaplain continued and then it came again. He looked over his congregation but all were tight-lipped. Several times the interruption was repeated. The preacher soared toward the climax of the sermon and in pictures described our Lord on his cross. Pointing to the imaginary painting he said, "In him is our only hope." As he said it he looked up and saw the lips of the old couple move in unison. This time, louder than before, they said simply, "Amen."

In some places services are interrupted frequently, even with shouts. Those who are used to a formal pattern of worship think it strange and are surprised when they hear it the first time. But this is the way some Christians use this simple little word. They agree with what they've heard. They like the way it was said, and to indicate their approval they say "Amen"—meaning, "You can say that again."

This is not an invitation to fill the church with "Amens" during the pastor's sermon next Sunday. We ought rather to know what the word means and how to use it properly.

"Amen" was originally a Hebrew word, although it has been adopted into almost every other language, with a variety of pronunciations. It is in Greek, Latin, Italian,

Spanish, French, German, Norwegian, Swedish, Danish, and English—to mention a few.

Its origin, as used in several places in the Old Testament, the Jewish Scriptures, was first and foremost liturgical. One finds it used among the Israelites as early as the exile in Babylon (Deut. 27:15-26 and Ps. 106:48). Thus it meant assent.

In the New Testament the writers of the Gospels use it in a slightly different sense and it is translated in some versions as "truly" or "verily." Thus in the Gospel of John we read in the Revised Standard Version (John 8:58), "Truly, truly, I say to you, before Abraham was, I am." Paul uses it many times.

Because of its use in the primitive church, "Amen," following the worship in the synagogue, came to be a regularly accepted liturgical word, and so has continued in Christian worship to this day.

In the liturgy it is first used following the Invocation—"In the Name of the Father, and of the Son, and of the Holy Ghost." In this instance, as in all others when the word is used in our worship, it should be said or sung with enthusiasm and intelligent agreement. It is more than the caboose on the train, more than a nice way to close a hymn or a prayer. It is the people's way of saying or singing, "We agree heartily."

We try to do just that. At least we sing it well, even if we may not always know what it means. There is one time, however, when we could give it more feeling. In the two orders for Public Confession, the pastor offers the Collect for Purity. At its conclusion, the word *Amen* is italicized, but few congregations respond with any amount of active participation. Perhaps it's because we sing "Amen" every other time, here we say it. Our response ought to be no less fervent here.

The same use ought to pervade all of our worship, particularly devotions at meetings of our parish organizations. Whenever prayer is offered in a group, even at the dinner table, all ought to respond with the word of assent. In hospitals, and at bedsides at home, at grace, at bedtime prayers—whenever we pray—all who are present acknowledge what has been said as theirs. We agree, our hearts are united, and with the one who prays we say "Amen."

At a discussion on worship, one man said he wished our people would learn to use "Amen" correctly. He said he felt the word was often mispronounced. When we sing it, it's usually "Ah-men," but when we say it, it's "Ay-men."

What shall we do? A famous singer from the Metropolitan Opera says he always uses "Ah-men" sung or said. A professor of liturgics disagrees. There doesn't seem to be a rule. This is hardly something to get excited about. The important thing is that the word be used intelligently, devoutly, enthusiastically. That means we must listen to what precedes our response. Our ears, our minds, and our hearts must hear, and having heard, we agree, "Amen."

CONFESSION AND ABSOLUTION

We who bear the name "Lutheran" have a guide in Martin Luther to whom to turn frequently. We read his writings, sermons, tracts, commentaries, not as a substitute for the Scriptures, but as a help that through his eyes we might see the things he saw.

One modern theologian has suggested that we must never think we understand any of Luther's thought until we have reduced it to the simple proposition: the forgiveness of sins through Jesus Christ. Every composition from the pen of Luther has this thought as its dominant theme.

It is not strange that the church has always stressed this central idea. Over and over again, in its teachings, we are reminded that the great message of the gospel is God's loving forgiveness. But it is not enough simply to teach this. It must be put to use.

Forgiveness of one's sin is not a teaching that one accepts or rejects. It is an assurance to a man weighed down by concern for his failures. When God says that he forgives our wrongs and our shortcomings, we receive his forgiveness. We do not just believe that the slate is wiped clean. It is.

This forgiveness is received in many ways, but it reaches its expression when, after having confessed our sins to God, we receive, as Luther says in the Catechism, "forgiveness from the pastor as from God himself. . . ." This brings to mind the promise of our Lord to the disciples, "Whose soever sins ye remit, they are remitted unto them; and whose soever sins ye retain, they are retained" (John 20:23).

In a Lutheran church the first part of the service is the Confession of Sins. We confess, using a general prayer in unison, all of the things which have separated us from God. Isn't this separation exactly what sin is? Then from the pastor we have heard the assurance of the forgiveness we seek.

These words of absolution, as we call the portion spoken by the pastor, have in the church's history taken several forms. Some churches, taking literally the words of Christ quoted above, have as a part of the absolution the words, ". . . and I forgive you all your sins . . ."

This is referred to as the indicative form. Another is the declarative form: ". . . I declare unto you the entire forgiveness of all your sins. . . ." This is the form which has found acceptance among most Lutherans in this country.

A third form is the prayer form. Generally the words employed in this pattern are ". . . may Almighty God forgive you all your sins. . . ." This form is found in most Protestant orders of worship, and is the one used by the Roman Catholic priest in the common confession which is a part of every mass. The indicative form ("I forgive you") is used by Roman Catholic priests only for absolution following upon private confession.

In the Brief Order for Public Confession in the *Service Book and Hymnal,* congregations have opportunity to select one of several forms.

Then shall the Minister say the Absolution according to one of the following forms.

Almighty God, our heavenly Father, hath had mercy upon

us, and for the sake of the sufferings, death, and resurrection of his dear Son, Jesus Christ our Lord, forgiveth us all our sins. As a Minister of the Church of Christ, and by his authority, I therefore declare unto you who do truly repent and believe in him, the entire forgiveness of all your sins: In the Name of the Father, and of the Son, and of the Holy Ghost. *Amen.*

Or

The Almighty and merciful God grant unto you, being penitent, pardon and remission of all your sins, time for amendment of life, and the grace and comfort of his Holy Spirit. *Amen.*

Or, where customary, the Minister may lay his hand on the heads of the penitents and say

By the authority of God and of this our office and ministry, I declare unto thee the gracious forgiveness of all thy sins: In the Name of the Father, and of the Son, and of the Holy Ghost. *Amen.*

On Sundays when the Sacrament of the Altar is not celebrated, the Confession of Sins is not omitted. Using a shortened form, sins are confessed and then the pastor speaking on behalf of God declares his gracious goodness to the penitent.

Some may argue that such diversity produces confusion of practice. That may be, but Lutherans in all of the bodies which use the book will find suitable expression given to the faith which puts at its center the forgiveness of man's sins through the sacrifice of Jesus Christ.

SILENCE

Most people who go to church simply pick up their books and "go through" the service. They know that things follow in a definite sequence, and all one has to do is to keep one's finger in the proper place for the Introit, Collect, and Lessons for the day.

Little attention is given by the average worshiper to how things are to be done. The General Rubrics, a sort of "how-to-do-it" section of the *Service Book and Hymnal* (pages 274-84), are for most people an unexplored territory somewhere in the middle of the book.

Here are directions to be followed in the Service, Matins, and Vespers, liturgical colors, calendar rubrics, precedence of festivals and days, and tables of Easter dates (from 1955 to 2002), movable festivals, lessons for Matins and Vespers, Psalms and psalm paraphrases. These directions ought to be known by all who use the book.

Chances are that most of our people will get to know some of these rubrics without bothering to turn to the pages cited. The men who prepared the *Service Book and Hymnal* took some rubrics from their hiding place and inserted them throughout the services. Thus, while it may take a little time for most of us to read the fine print as we move along in the service, we all ought to have a better idea of what we are to do next.

One pastor was particularly appreciative of this change, but he added, "Judging from the writer's experience in many parishes, double-sized italics, or perhaps red underlining would be helpful." Here he came close to the meaning of the word "rubric" itself. "Rubric" is derived from the Latin word meaning "red." In the ancient service books, while the text of the services was written in black, the directions were set down in red.

Care should be taken to note the verb in each rubric. Sometimes it is "shall," other times it is "may." "Shall" rubrics are considered as directive, and so constitute the basic structure of the service. By adhering to the "shall" rubrics, a congregation observes the "common rite authorized by the church."

The "may" rubrics represent a permissive use and are left to the determination of the local congregation. Thus in the communion service, the communicants in all of our churches are to be dismissed with the formula: "The Body of our Lord Jesus Christ and his precious Blood strengthen and preserve you unto eternal life," but not every congregation will sing or say the Nunc Dimittis afterward.

In the "Preface to the Liturgy" of the *Service Book and Hymnal* (p. viii) we read:

The Common Liturgy is rooted in the developed worship of the ancient and medieval Christian Church, both East and West, and grounded on the historic German, Scandinavian and American uses of the post-reformation centuries. Prepared especially for the use of Lutherans in the Western Hemisphere, the Common Liturgy presents the full Service of the Church with all its provisions for all who wish to use it. Essential material is preceded by a *shall* rubric; optional material by a *may* rubric. Freedom and flexibility in matters liturgical is our birthright, and there is room for ample variety in ceremonial, music, and architectural appointments. Some parishes may desire and have the resources to provide full and ornate services. However, the most ornate structure should not incorporate extraneous or un-authorized texts. Other parishes may desire or be able to provide only services of a simpler character. Likewise, the simplest service should not omit essential or important parts, or change their order. Every service, whether elaborate or simple, sung or said, should be within the framework of the common rite authorized by the Church, and its integrity should be respected and maintained under all circumstances and conditions.

One of the first of these rubrics comes in the Confession of Sins. Following the invitation to confession, we read: *"The Minister and Congregation may kneel."*

I suppose that almost every child who was taught to say his bedtime prayers knelt by his bedside. It was for most of us the most natural thing to do. But when we get to church many of us feel awkward about kneeling. We lean forward with bowed heads, hand resting on forehead, to say a prayer before the service. The kneeling benches, probably the most expensive pieces of furniture in our churches if one is to judge by the frequency of their use, are pulled out only for the public confessional services. Many American Lutherans have never knelt to receive communion, a practice which surprises most of our European brethren.

But the act of kneeling suggests humility, and where ought we to be more humble than when we confess our sins before God? Some will say that to kneel will not make even the proudest man any more humble, so why kneel?

Still the thought that I get down on my knees indicates to me, if to no one else, that I must humble myself before God. I bow before him who made me, before my Redeemer, before the Holy Spirit. I kneel in the presence of God and beseech his forgiveness.

Another rubric comes at the close of the confession. *"A brief silence may be kept before the Introit for the Day."*

Anyone who has watched television or listened to the

radio knows how distressing a pause of only a few seconds can be. Engineers in the studios, so I am told, are under intense pressure to be sure that every second is filled up. Something has to happen all the time.

This same sort of thinking has invaded our churches. That's probably why a lot of our people fidget during the long periods when the sacrament is administered. But this rubric, assuming it is observed, violates this practice. What it says in effect is: "Now let's stop our activity. Let there be utter silence in the church."

Of course this doesn't mean that we are all to sit and look at one another with anxious looks as if to say, "What happens now?" The reason for this rubric is that we are to be still for the briefest moment to think. How many of us ever do just that? We're all so busy jumping from one job to another, one problem to the next, that there is little time for thinking quietly about important matters.

This is a time to think of God. I've come to church for a purpose. I may not be fully aware of why I come, but the words and actions thus far in the service have caused me to think. If I give serious attention to what is said, I can't help but feel that I'm not the important person I suppose I am. The word "sin," my sin, has pulled me up short, and I get to thinking about me.

I've done a lot of things I ought not have done. Inconsiderate regard for others, selfishness, harsh words have all oozed out of me. And what about the things I didn't do? My forgetfulness, failures, inadequacies all come back to plague me.

Remembering these, I join those about me, and with my pastor I tell these things to God. Fortunately it doesn't end there. The pastor holds up the crucifix, figuratively at least, and pointing to it says: "God loves you. He has wiped the slate clean. Go and sin no more."

Whew! What a load is off my mind now. All that bothered me before is gone, and I can lift my head again. But should I stop there? That's where the brief silence comes in. If there is One who can take hold of me and change me from what I was to what I ought to be, and if I know that he has done just that, ought I not be thoughtfully grateful for his love? All around me are others who have had the same experience. Yes, things stand still that we may know God.

THE INTROIT

Just before Advent a pastor tried to explain to his children the meaning of the wreath on the dining-room table. He suggested that they try to draw a line that has no beginning or ending, hoping to get into a discussion about the circle as a symbol of eternity.

Tommy, who is in the first grade, thought about it for several moments, then said, "What about a circle, Daddy?" He got one of his crayons and a piece of paper to prove his point. His sister, who is four, took a look at the crude red egg Tommy drew and asked, "But where does it begin?"

A lot of people ought to ask that question about their worship. We go into church, bow for our prayer, watch the acolyte light the candles, stand to sing the first hymn as the choir and pastor enter the church, and then follow through with the service in the *Service Book and Hymnal*. But where does the service begin? To get our answer, we must turn back to history.

If you had attended a service in a church about thirteen hundred years ago, you would have entered a building much like many of our churches of today. While you knelt to say your private prayers, you would have known that the clergy and their assistants were doing the same thing in a small room near the front door of the church. In this room, called the sacristy, they donned their vestments and prepared themselves by prayer and meditation.

At the time appointed, the ministers and their assistants entered the church. At a signal, the first choir began to sing a verse from Scripture. This was called the "antiphon" and was usually taken from the Psalms.

As the procession made its way toward the altar, the second choir would repeat this "antiphon" (a Greek word meaning "to sound in answer"). Then the first choir would sing the first verse of the psalm appointed for that particular day. This was answered as the second choir and the congregation (who had now heard it twice) repeated the antiphon.

So it continued, the first choir singing the next verse of the psalm, and the second choir and the people singing the antiphon, and all the while the procession made its way up through the church. When all had arrived before the altar, another signal was given, and all sang the Gloria Patri.

When the Gloria Patri was finished, the antiphon was once again repeated by all, and the service went on from there. All this was called the Introit and comes from a Latin word which describes exactly what happens: "he enters."

In later years the sacristy was relocated just outside the wall of the sanctuary, thus eliminating the need for a lengthy procession. The ministers could enter without requiring a whole psalm to cover their movement from one end of the church to the other. Shorter portions of the psalms were sung, along with the antiphon. Eventually it became the practice to sing the antiphon once, a single psalm verse, the Gloria Patri, and the antiphon repeated.

This was the practice Luther knew. Although he recommended in his reformation of the mass that the ancient custom of singing a whole psalm should be followed, it soon became the custom of the many churches of the Lutheran Reformation to use the Introit as it had been developed. So it has remained to this day, except that in many places where the Common Liturgy is used the antiphon is not repeated following the Gloria Patri.

Thus our question is answered. What precedes the Introit is preparatory. The Introit is the beginning of the service.

Some churches have attempted a return to this custom. The choirs, except on festival days, take their places in silent procession. The pastor enters the church, stands before the altar rail, and conducts the confessional service.

There is a period of silent prayer. The pastor goes to the sacristy to vest, and then enters the sanctuary as the Introit is sung, going directly to the altar.

In many of our churches, this emphasis is maintained by the pastor conducting the confessional service outside the sanctuary, in front of the communion rail, and then ascending the steps to the altar as the Introit is sung.

These ceremonies may help, but it is important that the Introit be given great stress if it is to achieve what it is intended to do in our worship. The Introit is a hymn. It is meant to be sung.

A good preparation for Sunday's worship, whether at home or in the Sunday school which precedes the service, is to familiarize oneself with the psalm from which the Introit is taken. One may locate the psalm by use of a concordance, or by reference to *The Christian Year*.[1]

Find the Introit psalm and read it carefully. Try reading it aloud and perhaps, as in the seventh century, with the antiphon following each verse. Don't forget the Gloria

[1] Edward T. Horn III, *The Christian Year* (Philadelphia: Muhlenberg, 1957).

Patri. This is an ascription of praise to the Holy Trinity and should be said or sung after every psalm. This might well be a part of the devotions in the Sunday school.

When you read the psalm, relate its meaning to the Epistle and the Gospel for the day. Let all of them speak to you of the day being observed and of its significance for you.

A brief example may help. Christmas Day has two sets of Propers, one for an early service which is properly used on Christmas Eve (notice the Collect: "O God, who hast made this holy *night* . . .") and the later service for Christmas morning. The Introit for the later service has its antiphon from Isaiah 9:6, while the psalm verse is the first of Psalm 98. Read that psalm, repeating the antiphon (or perhaps just the first twelve words of the antiphon) after each verse, and notice how it relates to the incarnation. Doesn't the psalm take on new meaning and aren't the Epistle, Gradual, and Gospel made more intelligible? A theme has been sung and, by it, our worship begins in a new and different light.

KYRIE ELEISON

A pastor of a newly built church was once showing some of the members through the building. One man, pointing to a large X and P, asked what it meant. The pastor explained that XP represents the Greek word for Christ. The man replied, "I guess you've got to be a Greek to know what it's all about."

People may feel that way when they pick up the *Service Book and Hymnal*. Here and there are titles such as *Gloria Patri, Sanctus, Agnus Dei, Venite, Te Deum, Nunc Dimittis*. When told that these words are Latin, some people are perplexed.

The fact is that these are words used for more than a thousand years when Latin was the language of the church in western Europe. Our use of these words helps to make us realize our continuity with the church in ages past.

"Gloria Patri," for example, means "Glory be to the Father," and is generally used among Christians to indicate the doxology which follows psalms.

A few words we use go back even further, to the Greek language. The Greek word Kyrie (KEE-ree-eh) is the name for the sixfold antiphonal section following the Introit. Its fuller form is Kyrie Eleison and means, "O Lord, have mercy." Use of these words shows our connection with the days of the early church when, before Latin, Greek was the common language of the civilized world.

There is some doubt among scholars just how this cry for mercy became a part of early Christian worship. As early as the fourth century, a brief litany of intercession (a series of petitions for God's gracious attention) was sung following the assembling of the clergy in the church during the Introit. At the end of each petition, the congregation responded, "Lord, have mercy."

In the sixth century Pope Gregory discontinued this litany, but allowed a ninefold repetition of the age-old cry for mercy. A later change directed *Kyrie Eleison* be sung three times, *Christe Eleison* (Christ, have mercy) be sung thrice, and finally *Kyrie Eleison* thrice. (This is still the form, and in Greek, which is used in the Roman Church today.)

At the Reformation, Luther at first retained the ninefold form, stating that it be sung in Greek. Later he indicated a desire to use a form such as we know today, in the people's tongue.

In certain sections of Lutheranism, the Kyrie used to be sung following the Confession of Sins and was regarded as a musical response to it. This meant that the word "mercy" was penitential in character and so reflected in song the emphasis of the confession.

To overcome this misunderstanding of a word which has deeper meaning, it was necessary to find a form which would fit into the historic pattern of the service and at the same time eliminate any opportunity for penitential emphasis to be attached to the *Kyrie*. The result was to recommend a return to a modified form of the type of litany used in the early church. Thus in the *Service Book and Hymnal* the following is used:

In peace let us pray to the Lord.
    ℟. Lord, have mercy.
For the peace that is from above, and for the salvation of our
souls, let us pray to the Lord.
    ℟. Lord, have mercy.
For the peace of the whole world, for the well-being of the
churches of God, and for the unity of all, let us pray to the Lord.
    ℟. Lord, have mercy.
For this holy house, and for them that in faith, piety and fear of
God offer here their worship and praise, let us pray to the Lord.
    ℟. Lord, have mercy.
Help, save, pity, and defend us, O God, by thy grace.
    ℟. Amen.

As an alternate, the former use, if it is desired, may be
followed.

Too frequently, even among us, the Kyrie with its cry
for mercy has had a penitential association. It's as if we
went to church, admitted our failures and sought God's
forgiveness, received that forgiveness, sang the Introit, then
hesitatingly cast a backward look over our shoulders as if
to wonder whether we had really been forgiven.

In using the new Kyrie, worshipers will find a fresh
appreciation of the stages of our worship. Our first action
in church is penitential. That's the way it should be.
Coming into God's presence, we cannot help but be struck
by the comparison between him and ourselves.

God is totally different from us. He is goodness. We
know ourselves (if we are honest) to be full of selfishness.
Is it any wonder that worship must have its preparation in
penitence? So we confess, and with our expression of un-
worthiness comes God's gracious pardon. In spite of what
we are, God loves us!

We go on. The Introit is the place for song. This beginning of our worship sets the stage. We turn our thoughts
to one feature of God's goodness. We sing to him of the

event we wish to commemorate, adding our praise of this great God we worship in the trinitarian doxology. Then, instead of allowing doubt to creep in to plague us, we "come boldly unto the throne of grace," as the author of Hebrews (4:16) admonishes, "that we may obtain mercy, and find grace to help in time of need."

Look again at the petitions of the new Kyrie. The word peace occurs three times in the five sentence prayers. Unfortunately the word "peace" today has lost its savor. It means more than getting the Russians to behave themselves, or the Israelis and the Arabs, as a United Nations delegate said, "to act like Christians."

Peace doesn't mean only allowing Negroes and whites to sit together in schools, buses, and churches. Nor is it the peace of mind so popular in recent years. Peace is all this and a lot more. It is the quiet, calm assurance that God is with me and will guide me and love me always, and always invites me to rely on him. Dare one attempt further definition, particularly when the words which follow the sermon each Sunday are, "The peace of God which passeth all understanding . . ."? How can one explain it?

This is what we seek in the Kyrie. With humility, yet boldly; in appreciation for our own need, yet with confidence in God's love, we turn from ourselves to him, and with longing, joyful hearts we sing, "Lord, have mercy."

GLORIA IN EXCELSIS

In department stores immediately after Christmas the Christmas trees disappear and "January sales" spring up everywhere. It seems a shame that Christmas decorations go up before Thanksgiving but are ripped down on December 26. The church saves its celebrating until Christmas Day and then observes a period of almost two weeks to commemorate that wondrous event when God became man. We sing Christmas carols until January 6.

I don't think it sounds foolish to sing "Joy to the World" or "O Come, All Ye Faithful" while the world is putting away the Christmas decorations. In a sense I suppose I'm like the children who say they wish Christmas came more often. That's why I like the Gloria in Excelsis, Latin words meaning "Glory in the Heights." Even when the altar is banked with Easter lilies, or the temperature outside is a hundred in the shade, or we are commemorating the Reformation, when we sing the Gloria in Excelsis it's always Christmas.

Maybe Luther felt this way. He said that the Gloria in Excelsis "did not grow, nor was it made on earth, but it came down from heaven." Remembering the account of our Savior's birth in Luke's Gospel, one understands what he had in mind.

"And suddenly there was with the angel a multitude of

the heavenly host praising God, and saying, Glory to God
in the highest, and on earth peace, good will toward men."
Just as every Sunday, the first day of the week, is a com-
memoration of the resurrection, the singing of the Gloria
reminds us of the incarnation.

Christians have not always sung this great hymn as a
part of their worship. Like many of the hymns composed
in the early church, the Gloria began with a verse of Scripture, and was sung to praise God the Father. By the sixth
century it became a part of the first service of Christmas
Day.

Then it was used on all Sundays and on certain special
festivals. It was sung only by the bishops.

In the Middle Ages any priest celebrating a Sunday mass
was given the right to sing the Gloria. Luther retained it in
his first revision of the mass, but made no mention of it
in the second.

In some parts of Germany, because the music was difficult, a hymn composed especially for the occasion and
based upon the early form of the Gloria was substituted.
Thus the pastor would chant, "Glory be to God on high,"
the choir would respond, "And on earth peace, good will
to men," then all would sing the hymn, *Allein Gott in der
Hoeh sei Ehr"* ("All Glory be to God on High").

The Common Service, published in 1888, restored the
text of the Gloria in Excelsis to its earlier form. The *Service Book* directs (SBH, p. 274) that "the Gloria in Excelsis
shall be used on all Festival Days or when there is a Communion. At other times another Canticle or Hymn of
Praise may be sung."

In the *Service Book and Hymnal* a change from the
former pattern has been made so as to allow the pastor to
say or sing the opening words, and then the congregation
joins in the words beginning, "And on earth peace. . . ."

At first the Gloria in Excelsis was a hymn of praise to God the Father. It was later revised to include specific references to God the Son and a final section addressed to God the Holy Ghost. As we know it today, it is a hymn to the Holy Trinity.

Thus the Gloria came as a natural response to the Kyrie. One sees this even more closely when the new Kyrie of the *Service Book and Hymnal* is used. The litany-like Kyrie conveys the expression of humble reliance upon the mercy of God. Voices are lifted to beseech of God the blessings he desires to give us.

Then in trust that such gifts are truly ours solely because of God's goodness, there comes the expression in a triumphant hymn of our gratitude. You know how you feel when something really wonderful happens to you. It seems that words can hardly express your feelings.

It is unfortunate that for the most part we experience great joy only when we receive a personal gift or favor. God is given praise when we finally get a job, or when the baby recovers from an illness. Yet how much we ought to realize that God's gifts are far greater than even the things that make us happy, and that beyond the gifts we seek and obtain, and gloriously so, God is good!

How shall we speak of God? We use terms like goodness, truth, and beauty. But such words are abstract and do not help us to picture all of what we know God to be. It is not important that we imagine him in a certain type of robe, with crown and scepter, attended by all the pomp of a king. What is important is that we see, as far as we are able, just how wondrously good God is and then find some way to express the wonder.

In our worship, the Gloria in Excelsis offers just such a form.

Glory be to God on high!
And on earth peace, good will toward men. We praise thee, we bless thee, we worship thee, we glorify thee, we give thanks to thee for thy great glory, O Lord God, heavenly King, God the Father Almighty.

This is not saying "Thank You" for a specific gift. This is the expression which says in effect, "Thank God for God!" We praise, magnify, worship, glorify, thank God for what he is. It's not like treating a rich uncle with deference simply because we know that we might be mentioned in his will. It's more like the story that was told of the old woman who paraded up and down the streets with a torch and a pail of water. When asked what she was doing, she replied, "I'm going to burn up heaven, and quench the fires of hell, so that people will learn to love the Lord God for his own sake!" Glory be to God on high!

O Lord, the only-begotten Son, Jesus Christ; O Lord God, Lamb of God, Son of the Father, that takest away the sin of the world, have mercy upon us. Thou that takest away the sin of the world, receive our prayer. Thou that sittest at the right hand of God the Father, have mercy upon us.

The hymn of praise now turns our attention to God the Son. The gratitude we sang is now focused in him who died for us and sits at the right hand of the Father interceding for us. Here our thanksgiving becomes specific. Now our praise centers in the greatest gift of all time. God loved . . . he gave . . . whosoever believeth shall have eternal life. The only door to God's presence is Christ. Glory then to the Son!

For thou only art holy; thou only art the Lord; thou only, O Christ, with the Holy Ghost, art most high in the glory of God the Father. Amen.

Our destiny is not conditioned on an intellectual acceptance of what Christ did, as one accepts the law of gravity or the Pythagorean system. A person cannot reason out such matters in his mind and then say, "I believe." No, Another is necessary. Call him what you will—Spirit, Guide, Comforter—God is active in the world, and by the Holy Ghost you are moved to identify yourself with the truth that your mind of itself cannot accept. Glory to the Holy Ghost!

SALUTATION AND RESPONSE

For one who is well acquainted with the Bible, the words, "The Lord be with you," have a familiar ring. In the book of Ruth (2:4) Boaz goes into the fields and greets the reapers with "The Lord be with you." They reply, "The Lord bless thee."

The angel who greeted the Virgin Mary with the astonishing announcement that she was to bear the incarnate God said, ". . . the Lord is with thee" (Luke 1:28). And Paul concludes many of his epistles with just such a wish (compare II Tim. 4:22; Philem. 25, Gal. 6:18; and Phil. 4:22).

We expect to find such expressions in our worship, and usually take them for granted. Words get used so frequently, so often in a casual and unthinking way, that they lose the flavor they are meant to have.

When we leave a friend after even a brief meeting, we say "Goodby." This, as you know, is a shortened form of the ancient farewell, "God be with you." Does anyone really mean this parting blessing or prayer as he mumbles the conventional "Goodby"?

Words should have crispness, freshness, strength. Perhaps that is a reason why our teen-agers have a vocabulary all their own. These young people are beginning to get a hold on their thinking apparatus. They stand at the entrance of the adult world of responsibility, faced with much adult expression that is merely formal or meaningless. They have devised the use of recognized words for unique occasions to bring forth the vitality they so urgently desire. Words like "solid," "cool," "skin," "man," "square," and a host of others, placed in a strange background, stand out with an almost exotic difference. Just as an attractive lamp, a bizarre carving, or a tapestry splashed with brilliant colors placed in a room of a different style or period of decoration gives the whole room a richness unseen before, so words ought to force new meaning upon us.

Consider this simple little versicle, "The Lord be with you," and the response, "And with thy spirit" (which follow the Gloria in Excelsis), not so much for what it says, but as to its location. We divide our worship into two parts, which we call the sacramental and sacrificial. The first term describes those parts of the service in which God speaks to his people. To symbolize that the movement is from God toward man, the minister faces the congregation. Thus in the lessons and the sermon particularly God speaks to man.

The term "sacrificial" is the other side. An offering is made to God out of a thankful heart, without any thought of reward. In this classification are prayers, hymns, psalms, and our gifts in the offering. In our worship, in anything in which man makes an offering to God, the minister faces the altar as the symbol of God's presence.

Bearing this distinction in mind, that our worship is a sort of conversation between God and man, we see that "The Lord be with you" fits neither classification. This little insertion seems as though minister and people are for a brief moment talking between themselves.

In ancient times there was actually a brief pause in the liturgy and a sort of admonition was exchanged. In some of the Greek liturgies a deacon at times would stand in the front and shout, "The doors, the doors," or direct the catechumens, the penitents, and those under discipline to leave.

What followed was so sacred that only those who were in good standing as full-fledged members could be present. In effect, these insertions were like saying, "This is important; let's pay attention." At this point the Greeks were told, "Let us ask the Lord," or "Let us again and again ask the Lord."

In Egypt, a deacon would say simply, "Stand," or "Stand for prayer." What came later was perhaps more polite, but still was intended as an admonition. "This is special, get ready." One modern writer has suggested that it would be better if the minister were to say, "Brethren in Christ, we are going to pray." "Devout Christians, listen to today's Gospel."

So there is the interruption in our order of worship here before the Collect (which is the prayer for the day) also at the start of the Preface, and just before we are dismissed with the Benediction. The pastor turns from praising God, extends his arms (some say to symbolize that all we have and are is because of the cross), and says, "The Lord be with you." For this blessing the people stand and reply to the pastor, "And with thy spirit."

Notice that "thy" refers not to God but to the minister. Because this is the people's blessing upon their shepherd, the minister does not join the prayer, but stands before them in humility. Their words, incidentally, would have greater meaning were they to say, "And with you too."

All of this is to get us ready, a mutual exchange to sharpen our attention and make ready our hearts that we may make the words of the prayer the expression of our very own hearts, that we may enter fully into the moment of communion. We wish to know that we go forth with

God's blessing upon us. To this we add our prayer that we with our pastor may be truly united before God to receive his goodness.

The little phrase, "The Lord be with you," isn't intended only for use in the liturgy. Many groups are finding that they can add to their devotions if the leader will use the opening verse and all respond as we do in church. Not that it's essential, but isn't the use of the versicle a sort of frame to the picture? Perhaps if we use the words and think of their meaning in the service and outside, the intended effect will be felt by us. "The Lord be with you."

THE COLLECT

During election campaigns most of the candidates say something like this: "Give us your vote, get us elected, and we'll do great things for you. Put your trust in us, and we'll get what you want." Is it cynical to say that most of us don't expect that all of the promises will be fulfilled?

There is one promise, however, that many people know will always be kept. Never was there a promise like the one made by Jesus Christ when he said, "Whatever you ask the Father in my name, he may give it to you."

Christians know the value of this promise. Even the non-Christian has but to read the pages of history, since that memorable day when the promise was first spoken, to appreciate the power latent in it.

To be sure, the words are not a blank check. It isn't a matter of saying: Please, God, give me a thick bank book, a better job, or a mink coat, and then tack "in Jesus' name" at the end. People whose hearts have been opened by God's Holy Spirit know that this is not simply a formula or a magical incantation. Rather it is an attitude of our very being, an attitude which, by God's goodness, makes us live as if Christ lived in us, and so we ask in the spirit of Christ. This attitude we call prayer, and the precious promise which is so broad and so vast is our warrant for the petitions we raise "in Jesus' name."

One might expect that if Christians have such a fabulous treasure house at their elbow, they would unlock it frequently. If there is an assurance that such bounty is ours, then when we go to church, we must pray a lot. But do we?

If we remember that the Introit is the beginning of the service in our churches, isn't it strange that we don't really pray for quite some time? One writer has likened the situation to a call on a prominent dignitary. First we rub our shoes on the mat (confession), then we ring the bell (the Kyrie), then we greet him (the Gloria), and only then when we have done all these things do we bring up our requests.

Some people are confused when they see that the bulletin indicates "The Collect" following the Gloria. I once sat next to a Baptist friend who began digging in his wallet. He thought the time had come for the offering.

Actually the word "Collect" has a quite different meaning. In the early days of Christianity, it was the custom for all of the clergy of a town to gather with their people at a certain church. The church was designated as the station for that day, and the bishop offered a prayer which collected the petitions of the people, gathered them together.

Later, the term was continued to signify that the prayer "collected" the chief features of the day being observed. As the second of the five Propers for any given day in the church's year, the Collect frequently unites the theme which runs through the Introit, the Gradual, and the Lessons. Take time to study the Propers before attending a service and you will see the harmony pervading the variable portions of the service. All of them are united around a central event or idea in the life of Christ and his church. The Collect expresses that thought in prayer.

Scholars of Christian worship have been quick to recognize the beauty of these little prayers. In a few well-chosen words, they convey briefly, but completely, the petition which centers in the day's observance. Their beauty is heightened by the fact that they enjoy an "unbroken use of nearly fifteen centuries by multitudes of believers in all lands." [1]

Take one of them apart and you will find that they contain five main parts: the invocation or address, the antecedent reason, the petition, the benefit or fruit desired, and the doxology or conclusion. Sometimes the second and fourth parts are not present.

Because our Lord promised that our petitions would be granted if we asked the Father in his name, and also because his own suggested form was addressed to the Father, most of our prayers begin that way. This is not that we confuse the Persons of the Holy Trinity, or that Christ is not as truly God as are the Father and the Holy Ghost.

Of the proper Collects for the church year in the *Service Book and Hymnal,* one is addressed to God (for Trinity Sunday), ninety-one invoke God the Father, five call upon God the Son (the First, Third, and Fourth Sundays in Advent, Maundy Thursday, and the alternate for Ascension Day). There are no Collects among the Propers addressed to the Holy Ghost, although there is no reason why we cannot address our prayers to the Spirit, especially considering the words of such hymns as 117 in the *Service Book and Hymnal.*

There are many technical rubrics concerning the Collects. One who is interested in knowing more about how to use the Collects ought to take time to study them (see page 274 of the music edition of the *Service Book and Hymnal*).

The important thing is that we use these prayers as our

[1] Luther D. Reed, *The Lutheran Liturgy* (Philadelphia: Muhlenberg, 1960), p. 279.

own. True, it is the pastor who speaks them in the service, but the words he uses ought to be the expression of our hearts and minds.

One practical suggestion: why not use the Collect for Sunday in the week which follows? Every time you pray, add the Collect to your devotions. You'll find that soon its words take on a familiar ring and so are built in your mind the thoughts which permeate the time of the church's year.

Whatever the theme of Sunday's worship, you'll find that it comes back to you fruitfully during the week as you pray the Collect. Then, on Saturday evening as you prepare for the next day's worship, read the Collect for that day. You are ready to move on in the annual drama of Christ and his life upon the earth and in his church.

THE LESSON

One new feature in the *Service Book and Hymnal* follows the Collect for the day. At this point in the service these words appear:

Here the Minister may read the appointed Lesson from the Old Testament, saying: The Lesson is written in the —— Chapter of ——, beginning at the —— Verse. *The Lesson ended, he shall say,* Here endeth the Lesson.

Then may be sung a Psalm or a hymn version of a Psalm.

In the list of appointed Epistles and Gospels for Sundays, festivals, and holy days of the church year a lesson from the Old Testament is included.

Actually this isn't new. The *Common Service Book* (Music Edition, p. 291) says:

Before the *Epistle for the Day,* other Lessons of Holy Scripture may be read, but the *Epistle* and the *Gospel for the Day* shall always be read.

Perhaps it's because this rubric was buried that many of our churches failed to observe it. Regrettably most people seldom heard more of the Bible than that small portion which consists of the Epistles and Gospels for the church year.

Often we hear people say that we ought to try to do things as Jesus did them. In his day it was customary for people to attend the synagogue in their own village. As

49

a part of this service two lessons were read from the Hebrew Scriptures, one from the Law, another from the Prophets.

After each lesson, one of the members of the congregation would comment on the portion read. In Luke 4:16-21 we read that our Lord exercised this function in a visit to the synagogue in Nazareth.

After Pentecost, the Christians continued this practice. Later, letters written by the apostles were also read. These letters or "Epistles," as we call them, were admonitions from men like St. Paul or St. Peter and were addressed to certain communities.

Because the letters had an appeal to congregations other than those to which they had originally been sent, they were copied and circulated among the congregations. A reading of a portion of each letter at the assembly of the congregation soon became a regular feature of early Christian worship.

What we today know as the Gospels were introduced in the same fashion. At first the words of Christ and the events of his life were passed along orally. These accounts were eventually set down on paper and distributed throughout the church.

So, in early Christian worship, four lessons were read. Soon one of the Old Testament selections was dropped. Later the other was deleted also. Because the Lutheran order followed the rite of the Western, or Latin, tradition, our church in most areas had only the two New Testament lessons: Epistle and Gospel. Strangely enough, within the Church of Rome two of the ancient rites, which are observed only locally today—the Ambrosian and the Mozarabic—still retain the three liturgical lessons.

Religion may be popular today, but people don't really know Scripture. Difficulty in reading the older translations has something to do with it, but any person who feels that he can pick up a modern translation and breeze through it as he does his morning paper is deluding himself. Scripture needs not only reading but also study. And in a day when picture magazines and television occupy more of our attention than the printed page, Bibles gather dust on the shelves.

When this happens, when all that many people know are a few incidents in the life of Christ and only his most important words, when even familiar passages from Paul or John are heard less frequently than television commercials, man's familiarity with the things of the spirit is dulled and his relationship with God decreases.

One of the modern translations begins John's Gospel with "At the beginning God expressed himself." This is J. B. Phillips' way of paraphrasing "In the beginning was the Word." It is God's Word that informs us about God. The expression which falls on the ears of our minds and hearts is the door which opens up to us the unknown. And unless we listen to that expression, the unknown will ever remain a mystery.

So we listen to God's Word. In it he tells us about himself. He opens the curtains on what he wants us to know about himself and how we are to relate our lives to his. The eyewitnesses are gone. But their words, inscribed on the printed page, are the means by which we enter into a knowledge and understanding of God. The Gospels tell us of Christ, the Epistles explain what the Gospels tell, and the Old Testament lays the foundation for both.

It would be well for all to observe the rubric and read the appointed lesson from the Old Testament.

Pastors who conscientiously follow the pattern of the church year in the preparation of their sermons will be glad for the added strength that comes from the Old Testament lesson. As the prophecies associated with the Advent wreath help us to appreciate the coming of Christ, so by means of the other lessons from the Scriptures that he himself used, the background in the history of Israel will place in sharper focus the figure of him who came to men that by him men might once again be brought back to God.

THE EPISTLE

Anyone who gets a lot of mail is constantly seeking all sorts of short cuts to reduce the pile. "How can I say it fastest?" Only when I read through the neat stack placed on my desk for signing do I begin to feel ashamed.

In other days busy men wrote beautiful letters, carefully worded expressions which make us treasure their efforts. Their letters were not the flimsy, one-page, cliché-ridden forms we grind out today.

Of all the great letter-writers, St. Paul is unrivaled. His life would have been a nightmare to the modern, high-pressured executive. He was a traveler in a day when travel was not a matter of hopping a plane, an organizer whose efforts will be felt long after General Motors is no more. He was a mystic and scholar whose words penetrate the minds of men in every age.

He still found time to write letters. Wracked by bodily pains, burdened with the care of all the churches, Paul left his legacy in a small collection of letters, undoubtedly the most famous ever written.

Few could escape Paul's penetrating logic, his brilliant zeal, his compelling message. His whole personality, saturated with the grace of God, reached out to touch men, and once touched they were united with the apostle in devotion to the Savior.

Is it any wonder, then, that the early Christians, when they couldn't be with him or hear him preach, read his letters? That's what happened in the church. Although the letters were addressed to certain congregations, they soon were recognized as applicable for all. Copies were made and shared among congregations. In each assembly, along with preaching, prayers, and the breaking of bread, the "Christ-followers" heard again the words of the Special Messenger (that's what "apostle" means).

Long before the New Testament was put together in its final form, the Epistles (as we now call these letters) and the Gospels were known and loved by those who had become Christians. As the church grew, a varying number of Scripture lessons was read at the Sunday services, but always the Epistle and Gospel were read. It was the custom to read the entire Bible through over a period of time. Thus a reader would commence a certain book and read until given a signal to stop. When the church assembled again, the lesson was begun where it had ended before.

As Christian worship became more elaborate, the ministry developed into a seven fold progression. The priest or presbyter was permitted to preach and celebrate the mystery of the Lord's Supper. The deacon, once a helper of the apostles and later a candidate for the priesthood, read the Gospel and administered the chalice. Below him was the subdeacon. He read the Epistle.

The architecture of these early churches was similar in many ways to ours today. A raised platform at the east end was dominated by a large, almost square table or altar. Near by was the choir and beyond the altar, against the circular wall of the apse, was the throne of the bishops and the seats of the clergy.

The celebrant who officiated could stand in back of the altar, facing the people across it. In some quarters this plan is being introduced today. Between the altar-area or sanctuary and the nave were two *ambos* or reading desks. Much like our modern pulpits, they stood at opposite sides of the church. On the right, as one faced the altar, the *ambo* was lower and less ornate. The other, on the left indicated that its function was of greater importance in the church's worship.

When the time came for the lessons to be read, the subdeacon took up a volume called the *epistolarium,* containing all of the lessons to be read as the Epistles for the year. Proceeding to the *ambo* on the right or south side, he read the Epistle. When he finished the choir sang a psalm. The deacon then took up his book containing the Gospels (the *evangelarium*) and going to the desk on the left or north side read the Gospel.

In later years the *ambos* disappeared, and a pulpit was erected, usually on the left side closer to the nave. Lessons were then read from the altar, but the old tradition was retained. The subdeacon stood to the right in front of the altar to read the Epistle, while the Gospel was read by the deacon on the left. Some congregations follow this practice today and so perpetuate the old distinction of Epistle and Gospel sides of the church. The custom of reading both lessons from the lectern is a much later development, properly related more to Matins and Vespers and other services than to the chief service of the church, and came into American Lutheran usage largely in imitation of Episcopalian practice.

It is hard to say who determined the portions of Scripture to be read as the lessons for the year. Whoever was responsible, the lectionary (as the list is called) was accepted by Luther at the time of the Reformation. During the periods that followed, several attempts were made to revise the list or compile new ones. The *Common Service*

Book gave four additional lectionaries, three of which were German in origin (Thomasius, Hannover, and Eisenach).

In the *Service Book and Hymnal* the texts of the lessons are not printed. Because a decision could not be reached on whether to retain the King James Version or use the Revised Standard Version, it was thought best to include neither. Separate volumes, one with the text from the King James Version, the other from the Revised Standard Version, are available for use in the churches.

The Epistle is announced, giving the name of the Sunday, festival, or holy day. This is no place for embellishments, "stage directions," or pious ejaculations. The lesson is not "found in" or "taken from"; it "is written in." The rubric on page 3 is specific.

A good preparation for the coming day's worship is to read the lessons for that day. It is a good idea to compare the lessons given with the text in a modern translation of the Scriptures.

In our worship, following a period of praise and prayer, we turn to one of instruction. Having stood in respect for the presence of the God we worship, we now sit to be instructed. We have come before God, sung his praises, sought his favor, and now we are reminded of who and what it is we seek.

One writer says that in the Old Testament Lesson and the Epistle, God the Father speaks through his ambassadors. The Gospel is the voice of God the Son. And in the sermon God the Holy Ghost uses the lips of his servant.

So we listen and our ears catch the strains of familiar lines, lines taken from the letter of an old friend. What the ears hear, the heart loves, and the mind ponders. The words once set down by a brother in the faith become our words, and in those words God speaks to us.

THE GRADUAL

Some people are concerned about the kind of music used in the church. There seems to be a trend to intrude into the service music which isn't harmonious with our pattern of worship.

A study of the church's worship shows that, very early in its development, there was a place for special music. To be sure, the people sang, and we can imagine that it was a wholehearted, enthusiastic, joyous expression of their faith. But there was a place for the trained musicians. And in that place, they lifted their voices in a hymn which fit carefully into the theme and order of the day's worship service.

The subdeacon finished reading the Epistle from the *ambo* on the south side of the church and returned to his station. The deacon thereupon received the book of Gospels and after the ceremonies attached to his function, went to the north *ambo*.

All the while the choir sang its hymn, which united the liturgical lessons. The deacon and subdeacon, by their movements, were required to cross up and down over the steps which led to the altar. Because of this movement, the hymn came to be called the Gradual (from the Latin word, *gradus,* which means "step." One can appreciate

the meaning of the English word "gradually" in this connection).

The Gradual, then, as the only part of early Christian
worship allowing for special music, was thus functional.
It filled the period during which certain movements were
required by the unfolding order of the service. A lull was
filled with music by trained singers.

A modern parallel occurs in most of our parishes where
an anthem is sung during the reception of the offering.
Exhibitionistic tactics have defeated this function in some
areas by delaying the anthem, and in a few instances the
organ offertory, because, as I once overheard, "We artists
can't do our best when we are disturbed by the clink of
coins."

There are two parts to the Gradual. The first is the
Gradual proper, a verse or more, usually from the Psalms
(although some are from the New Testament and one from
an apochryphal book) which, as one writer says, "looks
back upon the thought of the Epistle." The second portion
is popularly referred to as the Alleluia. This, the same
writer indicates, anticipates the joyous proclamation of the
Gospel which follows it.

Alleluia is the Greek form of the Hebrew word meaning
"Praise ye the Lord." Among the early Christians, whose
language was the common Greek of the day, the word
was used as a cry of triumph or exultation.

Alleluia occurs frequently in the Psalter, and four times
in the Revelation of John. Particularly in the section
Psalms 113-17 (the so-called "Great Alleluia") does one
catch the full significance of this peculiarly religious word,
and so appreciate why it should have been adopted by the
church and used in its worship.

The Gradual was the bridge which united the thoughts
of the apostles with the words and work of Christ. The

hymn was assigned to the choir, but not always happily. It soon became the custom at times for a solo voice to sing the Gradual. Individualism began to assert itself. In 595 Pope Gregory the Great was forced to suppress solo graduals since, as he said, it had become customary for singers "to think more of their voices than of weightier things."

Another change in the form of the Gradual came later. Originally a brief composition of verses from Scriptures, the Gradual gave place to a lengthier composition known as the Sequence. Many of these works survived, later were translated and are now used as hymns in every section of Christendom. The *Service Book and Hymnal* contains several of them: "Christ the Lord is Risen Today" (99); "Come, Holy Ghost, in Love" (121) and "At the Cross, Her Station Keeping" (84).

With the elaborate musical treatment given to this lull, it was inevitable that the choir, then singing a lengthy narrative, should soon introduce features of the Greek drama. Soloists who represented scriptural characters began to act the parts assigned to them. From this, the medieval mystery plays developed.

Luther retained the classical Latin Gradual in his first revision of the mass, later allowed and encouraged (by composing several himself) the singing of appropriate German-language hymns. Following the Reformation, Johann Sebastian Bach composed cantatas inspired by those earlier sequences which were sung by choirs between the lessons.

The *Service Book and Hymnal* includes the texts of the Graduals from the traditional sources and designates that they should be sung by the choir.[1] If the Gradual is not used, a simple threefold Alleluia (in Lent a sentence is provided) or the seasonal Gradual may be used.

[1] General Rubrics (Music Edition), p. 275.

Certainly in some areas, particularly in mission congregations, it may be difficult to use the Gradual. The seasonal Gradual has been appointed for such situations. But its inclusion ought not be considered a warrant for omitting the Gradual. The Gradual is preferable. Only where circumstances prevent a worthy rendition of it should the seasonal Gradual be used. Anthems are not a happy substitute here, particularly when the text of the anthem bears no relationship to the lessons it is supposed to unite.

Music must serve the church. It must express accurately the faith we hold. The choir's part in worship is to lead the congregation, and at times to present appropriate special music. Before anything else the choir ought to sing the Gradual. It should give its attention to a careful preparation of it and then offer it as a part of the church's worship.

Thus the choir enjoys an opportunity to present its peculiar talent, not for the congregation's approval or for its own satisfaction, but as its worship of God. In so doing, the faithful singers in our choirs would well render an offering of their talents before the throne of the Almighty. At the same time the worshipers are helped to cross the bridge that links Epistle and Gospel.

THE GOSPEL

The living room echoed with a jumble of sounds. The television set boomed the virtues of a particular type of filter cigarette. The Lone Ranger and Tonto battled a range war full of the whine of bullets, the gallop of horses, and raucous shouts of "I've got you covered."

My wife and I were trying to have a brief conversation and several times I called for a cessation of hostilities. "I can't hear a word your mother is saying!" Then came the news broadcast which I wanted to hear, but the range war banged back and forth. Finally, in one of those moments of exasperation which only the parents of small children know, I declared, "Quiet! I want to hear what the man is saying!"

Strange, isn't it, how important certain words are at certain times! The weatherman's forecast may be a single strand in the volume of noise overwhelming us. But if it comes at a time when a long auto trip is in prospect, we listen with interest, not wanting to miss a word.

World tensions mount. Peace dangles precariously on the precipice. A man walks through the ranks of assembled legislators. "Shhh!" we say, "the President is speaking."

I can't help feeling overwhelmed by our failure to distil from this cauldron of sounds the only voice that is really important for us. Why do we sop up every syllable that gushes from the lips of government officials, industrial magnates, labor bosses, movie stars, and all of our other idols? Why is it that our ears will not screen out this volume of sound and permit us to hear the quiet, commanding voice of God?

Perhaps a lot of us suppose that when God speaks to us it must be out of the rushing wind, or with the deafening boom of thunder. It is frequently outside our conception of God that a street-corner evangelist, a humble church-school teacher, or even a poor preacher might be the broadcaster of the good news.

We spend much time trying to create a good impression. Our standards are contrived by the superlatives of modern advertising. It just doesn't seem right that God can and will do anything but in a big way. It isn't enough just to do something. We've got to put on a show.

I've never been able to escape such thoughts when I studied the origin of the ceremonies which go with the reading of the Gospel in our service. From as early as the fourth century there was a noticeable change in the proceedings at this point in the service.

The subdeacon had read the Epistle from the *ambo* on the left. Then, during the singing of the Gradual, the deacon (and no one in a lower order was allowed to perform the rite) received the ornamented and jeweled book of the Gospels. Acolytes took up lighted candles to stand on either side, and in later days incense was introduced.

The deacon, emerging from billowing clouds of incense smoke, proceeded to the north *ambo,* which was usually ornate. A stillness came over the assembled congregation. The people rose. Soldiers laid down their weapons. Even the king removed his crown. In an atmosphere of reverent awe, the Gospel was read.

Some of this ceremonial is still practiced among us.

Although we sit for the Old Testament Lesson and the Epistle, we rise, as a mark of reverence, for the Gospel. (It should be noted that the congregation ought to rise *before* the versicle which precedes the Gospel, not during it.) Unlike the other two lessons, the Gospel is framed by two brief sung responses, "Glory be to Thee, O Lord," and "Praise be to Thee, O Christ," which also serve to show our respect for what is read.

In a few of our congregations more elaborate ceremonial is encountered. Some have restored the ancient custom of a procession with lights, and a few use incense. I suppose such ceremonies help. The purpose of any ceremony is that it be a signpost pointing to a destination. Men remove their hats when they meet a woman. No one would argue that this in itself is anything but a mark of respect. If the doffing of a hat becomes only a custom without the attitude meant to motivate it, the custom is nothing.

When the Gospel is read, we are not simply hearing an account from history, as one listens to a retelling of Columbus' voyage, or of Caesar's wars. Rather it is the expression of God issuing from the words themselves which falls upon our ears and so, by the Holy Ghost, compels our hearts to respond.

This, in a very simple way, is an effort to explain what we mean by the Word. To be sure, this expression of God comes from every page of the Bible, as that page enlightens and expands the good news of God's goodness to us. But in the Gospel (which means "good news") this expression is most intimately related to the words and life of Jesus Christ. Thus God, who is the center of all, speaks to us.

Our ceremony, our rising to stand in silence, our voices lifted in song, are the actions we perform at this point in our worship to indicate our feelings. "Hush, this is important. It is the voice of God!" Our minds, which might have lingered over some far-off thought, our hearts perhaps embittered by some personal fault, are now to be focused and made ready. Emptied of our mental meandering and our emotional disturbances, we say, in effect, "Enter, Lord."

Then in the stillness, there comes the voice. In a sense we are transported back across the years, and we are at Bethlehem, by the Sea of Galilee, upon the hill of Calvary, in the garden.

It does not stop there. The picture formed in our hearts leads us along the path we call the Way. We react, as did the people of Jesus' day, to what we see and hear, and so make our response.

Dr. Luther Reed in *The Lutheran Liturgy* says that here in the reading of the Gospel is the "liturgical summit of the first half of the service, the office of the Word." Having come in our worship from confession and absolution, through praise, thanksgiving, and prayer, we stand, like Moses atop Mt. Sinai, waiting. The spoken Word fills the void, Scripture is read, a sermon preached. All of the noises of the world—to which our ears have long grown accustomed—are still. And through his Word, God speaks to us.

THE CREED

A couple of years ago a ballad entitled "I Believe" flooded the airwaves. It was full of allusions to raindrops, flowers, candle glow, the ever-present "you," and the inevitable "Someone." Certainly it wasn't a Christian creed, in spite of the fact that it was used in some churches as a junior choir anthem! But for a lot of people it is unfortunately an all-too-accurate expression of what they believe.

Any creed is simply a statement of one's beliefs. That's what "creed" means. But before a man is able to declare what he believes, he must be confronted with a fact, or group of facts.

Christ asked his disciples, "Who do you say that I am?" Peter's reply is one of the earliest of Christian creeds, "You are the Christ, the Son of the living God!"

Following the day of Pentecost, the church grew. People had to express their convictions. Creeds were prepared which believers affirmed at the time of their baptism. Several of these early creeds are known today, and it isn't hard to see how they were expanded to form the Apostles' Creed.

Creeds follow events. But oftentimes, although creeds have become established, a dispute arises about the events. Then it becomes necessary to restate the creed, or establish new ones.

The early church faced just such a crisis. A controversy

concerning the nature of Christ threatened to split it. In 325 a council of representatives from all over the church met in the city of Nicea, and there the debate was resolved with the adoption of a statement of belief which takes its name from the place of the meeting, the Nicene Creed. This form, revised at Constantinople some years later, is substantially the one we have in the *Service Book and Hymnal*.

Luther, in his first revision of the mass, continued the use of the Nicene Creed, although later he allowed the substitution of a hymn *("Wir glauben all' an Einen Gott")* in its place. Also, it was because of Luther, some say, that the word "catholic" was dropped, and "Christian" substituted for it. Actually the substitution occurred in Germany long before Luther's time. Properly, the word "catholic" means "universal" and was used to define one of the characteristics of the church. The German equivalent is *allgemeine,* and can also mean "general." Because this was awkward, pre-Reformation German Christians spoke of the *christliche* (or Christian) church, a practice which was continued by Roman Catholics in Germany even after the Reformation.

The word "catholic" belongs to Lutherans as much as to Roman Catholics, perhaps more so. Some Lutherans retain its use in their creeds. Swedish, Norwegian, Danish, French Lutheran liturgies use the word "Catholic," as does the *Manual de Culto Cristiano,* a Spanish version of the *Common Service Book* for use in Latin America. In the *Service Book and Hymnal*, permission is given to substitute the word "catholic" for "Christian" in both of the creeds.

The Creed is our response to God, not a mere recitation of events of history. God speaks to us through his Word. His words are the piercing, burning summons reaching into the depths of our innermost self. As a mark of our tribute to the presence of God with us, we say with conviction, "I believe in one God. . . ."

That is why we have creeds. The Apostles' and the Nicene creeds are our way of affirming our faith in God's good will for us.

We ought to learn to use the Creed. In our churches we should be careful to say it properly and with a conviction born of our appreciation and understanding. Some people recite it with the same unconcern as did the little boy praying the Lord's Prayer who said, ". . . and lead us not into Penn Station."

Look up pronunciations and meanings in your dictionary (for example, "Pontius" is pronounced like "conscious"). Note the punctuation.

For your devotions, try taking the Creed apart. Each portion is a window which looks out upon a whole landscape of God and his concern for us. During the offering or some other lull in the service, meditate on the Creed instead of gazing around the church. Each Sunday let your mind dwell upon all that each part of the Creed means to you. You'll find fresh delights facing you.

The general rubrics of the *Service Book and Hymnal* direct that the Nicene Creed is to be used on all festivals and whenever there is a communion (p. 275). The Apostles' Creed, the rubric continues, is to be used at other times. By festivals are not meant simply Christmas, Easter, and Pentecost, but all of the days listed on page 278.

It is apparent that many people don't know the longer of the two creeds. The Apostles' Creed they can say with books shut. The other must be read. Perhaps with a more frequent use it too will be known and so loved by all of us.

Another suggestion, now in use in only a few of our churches, is the singing of the Creed. The words we sing stick with us much longer than the words we speak. There are several good musical settings of both creeds.

Why not try to sing the Creed for a particular festival, perhaps Trinity Sunday? The setting can be inexpensively mimeographed. Sunday and weekday schools can devote a few minutes of each session to its preparation. On the day appointed the entire parish will unite in song in its confession of faith.

A few years ago a small book attracted a lot of attention. Containing the brief statements of prominent people, it attempted to put before the reader what they believe. It was a disappointing collection of vague references, with few mentioning God, and even fewer owning up to any formal religious conviction.

This is the voice of our times. We who hear the voice of God have our answer, and dare not keep it to ourselves. Against such sentimental vagueness, today's Christian must declare boldly, "I believe in one God. . . ."

THE HYMN

Just before the start of a World Series game or a large political rally the audience hums with the small talk of a thousand voices. Over the loudspeaker, a voice rises above the babble: "Ladies and Gentlemen, the national anthem."

People rise from their seats. Men remove their hats. Silence falls. A beautifully dressed woman (sometimes it's a man) fills the place with the ringing majesty so familiar to us all. "Oh say, can you see . . . ." Patiently the assembly maintains a respectful silence through the rapidly changing melody. The singer reaches a mighty climax—". . . and the home of the brave!" The notes trail off on the distant air and the people settle themselves for the program before them.

Why is it that no one ever joins in the singing? Most Americans learned the national anthem as children. Singing it was a part of every school day. Certainly "The Star-Spangled Banner" isn't an easy melody to sing. But this isn't an excuse. Have we become such a nation of watchers and listeners that we expect people to do things for us?

We just don't sing the way people once did. The teenagers perhaps are the exception. They know all the latest tunes on the Hit Parade. Little children sing too. Our house rocks after bedtime with a curious mixture of every kind of song—hymns, television commercials, folk songs, popular hits.

But for the rest of us, the old thrill of a group of men and women lifting their voices in song is largely a thing of the past. "We feel too self-conscious," we say. "I can't carry a tune." "The melody's too high." Excuses all, and we're missing a lot of pleasure.

One of the joys of my youth was to sit with a group of men and women in the summer evenings and join in melodies that are almost forgotten today. There were rich voices, clear sopranos, soft altos, strong tenors, deep basses, and the harmony at times, so I thought, was good.

There were a lot of other voices too, voices that simply carried the melody, voices that screeched a little, or that sharped when they should have flatted, but the chief thing was to watch the faces of the people as they sang. They weren't acting. Few would have dared to stand before an audience. But for them it was fun.

Unless one is fortunate enough to share in such happy gatherings, the average fellow who isn't a member of a choir or a chorus seldom gets a chance to sing. Even in church, where music is such an important part of the service, many people don't sing. They're afraid of what the person alongside will think.

I suspect they'd like to sing. The man who timidly mouths the words of a hymn for fear of making a spectacle of himself would thrill if he could open his mouth wide and lift the expression of his heart to God on the wings of song.

Wouldn't it be a good idea to encourage group singing in our parishes, not simply at the service but at all our congregational functions, if for no other reason than to break down the wall a worshiper builds about himself when he comes to services?

Lutherans are conservative, so much so that at times our

Methodist and Baptist friends say we're too close to the Roman Catholics. In matters of doctrine, we're sometimes called "thick-headed." We are also called the singing church, and our history proves that the Reformation message often found its strongest expression on the wings of song. A few days spent with our Scandinavian brethren will convince anyone. Swedes and Norwegians use any excuse to sing, and their singing is a joy.

One of Luther's chief contributions to worship was the inclusion of hymns, some of which he wrote himself, in the structure of the mass. Preaching might not always break through into the understanding. The liturgy with its impressive ritual might appeal to the eye, but be lost to the heart. But when the fundamental truth of Luther's recovery of the gospel was set to song, few could escape its influence.

Pastors who have been called in at the last moments of a dying immigrant know the affection in which many of these old hymns are held. A friend of mine told me that his grandmother looked into the faces of her loved ones as they stood about her death bed. "Sing," she said, "sing please *Wer nur den lieben Gott lässt walten* (If thou but suffer God to guide thee)." Slowly her son began the melody and the others took it up. In that little room a group of Christians brought comfort to a dying person and, in their song of faith, to themselves.

Other churches, recognizing the contribution made to religion in congregational singing, adopted it too. Roman Catholics, many of whom claimed that song had done more to make Lutherans than all of the preaching of the Reformers, copied the idea.

The result is that today there is hardly a service in a Protestant church which does not include hymns, and while hymns are seldom sung at mass in Roman churches, other services make provision for the people to sing.

The *Service Book and Hymnal* contains 602 hymns. It is embarrassing to ask how many of these are known and sung by the local congregation. And yet congregations and pastors ought to be embarrassed. One soon gets tired of a steady diet of the same thing.

To sing nothing but the familiar hymns of Keble and Watts, Sunday after Sunday, makes a person want to cry for one of the old chorales. To sing nothing but chorales can be equally tedious. Certainly there are enough hymns in the hymnal so that a pastor or choir need never lament for more.

But to have over six hundred hymns in front of us isn't going to make us sing. Group singing ought to be encouraged throughout the congregation: at the services, in the schools, and the meetings of auxiliaries and committees. And why not open church council meetings with a hymn?

Enthusiasm should be carried over into the home, and parents would do well to teach their children the hymns of the church. Still there is that large body of members whose only contact with the church is on Sunday morning.

Why not a brief hymn-sing just before the service? Let the choir use an unfamiliar hymn as an anthem for a few times. Then at the hymn-sing, pastor and people can practice. Someone ought to lead, even with a cautious bit of arm-waving if for nothing more than to give the beat. When some portion of the hymn sounds as if it needs improvement, stop the singing and start over again, working on it until it is right. Let the whole congregation take part in an enlarged rehearsal. Congregations will be surprised at the result, and the scowling faces one usually sees when a strange hymn is announced will be no more.

Pastors can do something else about hymns. The liturgy

calls for two hymns at least. Hymns shall be sung before the sermon and following the General Prayer. These are required (note the rubric). The general rubrics *(Service Book and Hymnal,* p. 274) direct that "A Hymn of Invocation of the Holy Ghost, or another suitable Hymn, *may* be sung at the beginning of any service. . . . A Hymn may be sung after the Benediction at any service." Two hymns are required, the others are permissive.

The hymn before the sermon is the chief hymn of the service *(Hauptlied),* and should be chosen carefully by the pastor to harmonize with the propers of the day and point to the sermon which follows. Of course this means that the sermon ought to relate to the thought of the day.

It isn't difficult to select an appropriate hymn for any occasion. An index in the SBH is of great help to one unfamiliar with the hymnal. The hymn following the Prayer of the Church, while it has been dropped in some congregations, is necessary and serves to indicate the end of a particular part of the service.

Pastors can also insist that the congregation have an opportunity to sing whole hymns. There ought be no announcements like, "Let us rise and sing the first, third, and fifth stanzas of Hymn 202." Each hymn is a unit of expression and a portion of its thought is lost if stanzas are omitted.

How absurd it is to sing only the first stanza of "A Mighty Fortress." Such a use of Luther's Reformation hymn leaves the world in control of the devil. Nor should congregational singing be suppressed while the choir sings a stanza in the narthex. Congregations ought to rise and begin singing on the first note. The same is true of the recessional. I know a pastor who dislikes the custom of congregational singing fading away as the choir leaves. To show his opinion he continues to sing lustily through the

Amen. A few more such individuals may help our singing.

The psalmist urges, "O come let us sing unto the Lord a new song." We've got to learn to sing the old ones, first, then the new ones. Why not try it on Sunday?

THE SERMON

One of my favorite weekly chores has been to read the church notices in Saturday's paper. Sensationalism in advertising isn't restricted to breakfast cereals, cigarettes, and automobiles. Some of the "live-wire" clergy have long since broken out of the quiet little box that announced simply the hours of worship and the location of the church. Advertising is as essential to the progressive administration of the parish as once were bazaars, festivals, and suppers.

One cleric, whose "copy" should insure him a job in any advertising firm, if he ever decides to stop "selling" the church, tickles the imagination. One "ad" read something like this. "See our beloved minister in his flaming red cassock! Hear him preach, 'From Hell!'"

Evidently this wizard succeeds, for the other notices, though not so large, show the same sensational tactics. Just read the sermon titles! I have often wondered if there are some people who scan Saturday's list and pick their church for the Lord's Day much as one decides which movie he'll see. And are there those who select the service on the basis of whether the pastor or his assistant will preach? Does one go to church because the sermon subject arouses his interest?

To say "preaching is important" misses the point. The church's lifeblood is preaching. Christ commanded it. The apostles established it. In every age the church's greatest advance resulted from it. Captivated by the irresistible brilliance of the good news (that there is a God who does care what happens in the world—so much so that he came here himself), inflamed by the compelling urgency of One whose voice speaks to man's innermost self, men have found their minds to be obsessed, their hearts ablaze, their words convincing. So the voice of God is heard in the world. This is preaching and without it there can be no church.

It is strange therefore that in a day so full of immorality on one hand and religious popularity on the other, the potent weapon of preaching has such little effect. Why, in spite of the list of varied subjects advertised from pulpits across the land, and as part of our radio and television diet, do crime, mental sickness, and marital infidelity soar to new records?

Why, with a larger church membership exposed weekly to the preaching of our pastors, is there no marked effect upon piety? Are the pew-sitters being lulled to complacency by platitudes? Are the sermon subjects unrelated to life? Is religion being sold as a sort of heavenly life insurance? Do preachers talk over the heads of their people? Are they fearful lest they offend a prominent member?

Many questions are being asked in many quarters. For every question there are several answers. Some will say that the already-crowded schedule of the pastor affords little time for serious sermon preparation. Others contend that too much emphasis is put upon externals—the sacrament is magnified and so the sermon suffers.

"Imagination, experience, reason are missing," a layman laments, "and Sunday after Sunday I get the same pat formula, 'Jesus is the answer.' I get so I want to stand up and yell 'Why?'"

Before anyone criticizes preaching today, he ought to

know what happens when he goes to church. What should a person expect when he attends a service?

First, there is anticipation, marked by the confession and God's forgiveness. This is followed by praise and prayer. Then God speaks to us. From the pages of the record of people like ourselves, their experience, their witness are conveyed to us.

The Lessons from the Old Testament and the Epistles and the Gospels are voices out of the past but, in a real sense, voices which are timeless. Our ears hear the voices of men, but our souls receive the voice of God.

Then the pastor enters the pulpit. He is not there to offer his opinion, to say "it seems to me" or "in my opinion." We have not come to hear the views of a particular person. With firmness, with zeal, with loyalty, the servant of God stands in the midst of his people with only one message— *Thus says the Lord!*

It is God's Word you have come to hear, not man's. If the preacher is true to our sequence of worship, the message will unfold the truth which comes from the day's Propers. His theme may dwell upon one of the Lessons, the Introit or the Gradual, or it may be a synthesis of them all.

But if he is conscientious the sermon will amplify the event or teaching of that day within the cycle of the church year. The wisdom of such an arrangement becomes obvious when one considers that within the course of a year, the whole cycle of God's love is re-enacted for man's growth in grace.

Nor will the sermon be exhortation only. Television commercials don't just repeat the name of the product. They tell you why you ought to try it. They explain its features. So as one listens to the sermon, he will have to expect that he must think!

The worshiper will find that his heart responds. God's

Spirit is busy within as he lubricates the gears of our brain, softens the hardness of our heart, and by a word or two those gears are set in motion, that long-pent-up impulse to love and to serve is unleashed. God is speaking to us. Don't turn him away.

Something else will happen. Remember how we watched our teachers show us how to draw, to sew, to write, to use tools. How eager we were to try it ourselves.

So when God speaks to us, we are compelled to act. As with the Ethiopian to whom Philip preached, baptism comes first. Confirmation—the ratification of our baptism—follows, and then regularly, frequently, the blessed communion with the risen Lord becomes our spiritual food until that glorious day when the veil is dropped and we stand before him who long before called us to be his own.

There are many kinds of preaching. Our concern here is with that preaching which forms a part of our customary weekly worship, "liturgical preaching."

In Judaism, sermons followed the reading of the Torah, and were a commentary upon it. Some believe that Ezra and the Levites were the first preachers and that their preaching began as a liturgical development. The sermon was an integral part of the liturgy.

We know of the continuance of such practice in the days of Jesus (Luke 4:16-30). Our Lord read the lesson from Isaiah 61 and then preached on it. Notice that while the lesson was read standing, the preacher sat. This custom was followed in the days of the early church when the bishop sat behind the altar and spoke to the congregation in a friendly, intimate fashion, as one does in a family gathering. Only at a later date did the sermon cease to be a conversational address and become a formal discourse.

Whatever the form, one thing was certain. The sermon presented the gospel. "We preach Christ," as Paul says, "and him crucified." An early Christian martyr tells that when the people met, among other things, lessons were read, "the president verbally instructs and exhorts to the imitation of the good example," and the Lord's Supper followed.

From a very early time, preaching and communion were always united. There was seldom if ever a purely preaching service as we know it today. The ordered sequence of lessons and other propers developed the church year, and by sermon and sacrament the people were united with God.

A period of decline followed. Sermons became subjective. Much emphasis was given to "living a good, clean life." The established order of service became a formal thing. Mass could be said without a congregation. No longer was what happened in the church each Sunday related to life.

Luther brought about a change. Preaching was restored to its rightful place in worship. Some people feel that Luther brought back the Sunday sermon as a substitute for the liturgy. They cite his directive that the people were not to assemble unless "God's Word is preached."

Such a view distorts history. With Luther it was not a question of "sermon *rather than* liturgy" but *"both* sermon *and* liturgy."* Moreover he specifically insisted that preaching on Sundays be related to the Gospel appointed for the day. Thus the ancient pattern was restored, and once more by sermon and sacrament the people were united with God.

Not all of the Reformers followed the lead of Luther. Zwingli substituted a preaching service for the mass, and ordered that the sacrament be celebrated but four times a year. Calvin, although inclined to follow Luther's example, was unsuccessful in establishing his ideas, and the preaching service became for Calvinists the regular form of Sunday worship. The influence of this innovation is still evident in Reformed and Presbyterian churches, although now the trend in both of them as well as in most Protestant bodies is to follow Luther, not Zwingli.

The influence of Zwingli affected Lutheranism, and with the coming of Pietism (a system which placed much emphasis upon personal devotion and morality) and later Rationalism (which subjected the gospel to a rigid scrutiny limited by man's ability to reason), the truly liturgical balance of sermon and sacrament suffered. Under Pietism, one went to church to be scolded into being good and under Rationalism to be lectured on subjects such as animal husbandry and philosophy. God and life were no longer united in worship.

Within recent decades efforts have been made to restore this balance. With the return to the historic form of worship employed in the days of the church's greatest vitality, men have been taught to unite in worship which is meaningful only as it brings them before God.

The observance of the church year with its annual re-enactment of the life of Christ upon the earth and in the hearts of the faithful has influenced preaching to the extent that sermons over the period of a year can provide the whole cycle of all that man needs to know about God.

With the growing appreciation of all that Holy Communion means, man is given the opportunity to respond to God's Word in the sermon so that the living bread of heaven is available when he feels the need of it. From this restoration of the balance between sermon and sacrament, as they are related to man's life, the Christian awareness of God and his submission to the Almighty is given greater opportunity for fulfilment.

To summarize:

First, liturgical preaching (that is, preaching within the

framework of the chief service) is discourse on the good news of Jesus Christ by one called as a minister of the church of Christ to his fellow-members of the church. It is an address among the members of a family which sets before the assembly the truth of God as revealed in the words and work of Jesus Christ.

Second, this preaching in its fullest sense is a liturgical action in the complete service which includes the giving of Holy Communion and is so integrated within the service as to have a proper place, time, and thought.

Finally, and conditioned upon the first two, such a sermon is the bridge which connects man in his modern, hurried, consuming life with the eternal Word of God, Jesus Christ.

When a sermon fully embodies these three features, then the Votum which concludes the sermon is a fitting benediction on all that has gone before. The worshiper has come through a period of anticipation and approach into the presence. Arrested by the voice which speaks to him out of the thoughts of those who went before, he has had those words amplified so as to penetrate to the center of his innermost self. Comforted when afflicted, afflicted when comfortable, he knows that God has spoken to him and out of that message there comes peace, God's peace which passes all understanding.

THE OFFERTORY AND OFFERING

It used to be the custom for the pastor, after completing his sermon, to raise his hand in blessing and say the Votum: "The peace of God which passeth all understanding. . . ." The people rose and replied to it with the Offertory, in most cases the familiar "Create in me," from Psalm 51.

Then they sat down and the ushers took up the plates to receive the offering. During the interlude the organist played a voluntary and the choir sang an anthem. The offering was then brought to the altar and the people stood again for the General Prayer.

This procedure made of the Offertory a response to the sermon, thereby detaching it from its rightful association with our offering. Some congregations, feeling the need for a congregational response at the time of the offering, inserted the doxology, "Praise God from whom all blessings flow," or "All things come of Thee, O Lord." A few added a short prayer that God would bless these gifts, and then followed it with the longer General Prayer. None of these practices, while seeming to correct an obvious omission, was quite satisfactory.

The *Service Book and Hymnal* directs that following the sermon the people shall rise for the Votum and respond to it with an "Amen." Then the offering is to be received "and presented *at* the altar."

Notice that the rubric says, *"at* the altar." This allows the pastor to receive the plates from the ushers or the acolyte and hold them before the altar until after the singing has ended, then place them on the credence table. This custom, some insist, fulfils their understanding that only the altar missal and the sacramental vessels should be allowed to stand on the altar.

Another rubric directs that when the sacrament is celebrated, the pastor shall prepare the communion vessels during the singing of the Offertory.

After the Offertory has been sung, the minister then offers the Prayer of the Church.

The wisdom of this arrangement becomes apparent when one studies the history of the offering as it had developed in the liturgy. Originally the people, complying with the word of Paul that gifts are to be offered on the first day of the week (I Cor. 16:2), brought to the church many different kinds of offerings.

Foodstuffs including bread and wine, as well as money, at this point in the service, were carried by the worshipers in procession to a table placed near the altar. The deacons then took charge of these gifts, arranging for their distribution to the poor, and a portion of the bread and wine was set aside for the sacrament which followed immediately.

Later this offertory procession was changed to a purely ceremonial function in which the deacons, no longer the lay assistants to the minister but now a lower grade in the order of the clergy, carried bread and wine from the sacristy or from the credence to the celebrant at the altar. Alms were collected at the church door. Thus the people lost their sense of participation in response to God's Word.

In post-Reformation times the ceremonial offertory procession disappeared. Bread and wine were set upon the altar before the service. While provision was made in some quarters for the offering of the people at this point, the practice was never fully developed to the extent we know it today.

In recent years the church's emphasis upon stewardship, as that term relates to the Christian's offering of both his gifts and himself, has given greater significance to that part of the service called the Offertory, the whole section of the service which includes our offerings, the sung response, and the Prayer of the Church.

God's Word demands a response. When one places an envelope or a bill upon the offering plate, is it regarded only as part of a payment for the pastor's salary, the lighting and heating of your church, a foreign missionary or a new building? Is it simply paying one's share of the bills? Or is it an expression of one's commitment to Christ? Are the coins and bills put on the offering plate a return to God, the best we can offer, of all that he has given us?

With such an understanding, the worshiper can appreciate that in effect he is offering himself to God when those plates are returned to the altar and offered to Him.

Yet think how a churchgoer must feel when he knows that only a handful of the envelopes are returned to the altar as a token of that dedication. This happens in some churches. Plates are hurriedly emptied into a basket in the narthex, leaving a few envelopes to symbolize the total offerings of the congregation. The larger portion is rushed to the basement or the parish house and the ushers begin to count so that they won't have to stay so long after church. If I were a member of a church where this happened I would protest vigorously; all of the envelopes ought to be brought to the altar!

Some other practices relating to the offering need investigation. It's time we got rid of the pile of shining brass plates, or at least look for a more suitable substitute. This is not to suggest that the offering be received at the door as one enters the church. Our offering is a part of the service. By it we respond to God's Word.

But, with the increased use of envelopes, plates are piled high. The solution accepted by some is to purchase more plates, and the result is a towering stack upon the altar or credence table. I once saw such a pile teeter precariously during the General Prayer, arresting everyone's attention except the pastor's, only to have the leaning tower crash to the floor with a deafening clatter just before the prayer ended.

The Germans have a vessel that looks like a coffee pot, frequently with two handles, and a slot on the top for the worshiper's gift. Some Anglicans use an embroidered bag suspended from a metal hoop with two handles which is passed from person to person. What one youngster called "popcorn poppers" — baskets or plates affixed to long handles—which are handled only by the ushers, are used in most Roman Catholic churches.

In one church all of the offering is emptied into two large embroidered brocade bags which are placed upon the two larger alms basons and borne to the altar by two of the ushers.

But whatever device is employed, two features are essential: the worshiper must be permitted to make his offering in the service as a response to God's Word, and all of the offerings must be presented at the altar.

The same could be said of the offerings of the Sunday school. Are they not a part of the total gifts of the parish? Sunday school officials may not agree, for this implies a unified treasury for the congregation. But why not present these gifts at the same time? This implies that the school is not a unit in itself, but is the educational department of the parish. Therefore the commitment expressed in one's offering in the school is symbolized by its presentation at the service.

Another feature, recently introduced in a few of our congregations, is to restore the offertory procession. In addition to the presentation of gifts of money, bread and wine are also brought to the altar, usually by a man and a woman chosen by the pastor, and presented as symbols of the other gifts we make. Care must be taken that this does not become merely a pretty ceremony but that it dramatizes that God uses the gifts we bring as vehicles of his grace. Our money supports and expands the church's ministry. Our bread and wine become for us the communion of the Body and Blood of the Lord.

This is the significance of the Offertory. Christ is the Vine, we are the branches. He is the Head, we are the members. His efforts to win us and sustain us, and to reach out beyond the limitations of our particular parish, are strong only insofar as we will return to him what is his alone.

The church will always be limited by the willingness of its members to remember their obligation to return to God all that he requires to accomplish his purpose. A Christian dare not hold back. The horizons of the church are limitless, the world is its goal. Our commitment must be entire.

PREPARATION OF THE ELEMENTS

Drama is a combination of words and action. Costumes, music, and settings may be added for effect, but speech and movement are indispensable. Someone has compared the church's worship with a kind of sacred drama. In the average parish church at its Sunday worship there are many movements: the procession of choir and minister, the moving about of the minister from lectern to altar, the turning to and from the altar, the reception and presentation of the offering by the councilmen, and of course our varying postures—kneeling, sitting, and standing.

In addition, though less firmly affixed to the liturgy, are other movements: the lighting and snuffing of the candles (in most of our churches a good illustration of overacting), and the usually zealous performance of ushers guiding worshipers to seats.

Notice that in the service the words are primary. Actions, for the most part, are incidental. These actions serve a purpose and so are related to the words they accompany: for example, the pastor's turning to and from the altar to indicate the sacramental and sacrificial divisions of the service. Facing the altar, he is our spokesman before God. Turned about, he speaks for God to us.

At one point of the service however a functional movement takes place which is not identified in any way with the script of the drama. In the *Service Book and Hymnal* there is this rubric: "When there is a Communion, the Minister, after Silent Prayer, and during the singing of the Offertory, shall uncover the Vessels and reverently prepare for the Administration of the Holy Sacrament" (p. 5). Another rubric (p. 275) amplifies this direction.

This action of the minister is important. It has to be done if the service is to be completed and the people receive God's gracious gift. Yet it seems that at this point one of the actors says his lines silently, and performs several little actions privately. The rest of the cast meanwhile lifts its voice in song.

Isn't there something wrong with our drama that "hides" these words and actions under the "lines" of the other actors? Is what he does and says so unimportant as to look secretive?

In the section on the Offertory I stated that in the early church the people brought their gifts to the church and after the preaching carried them to a small table near the altar. These gifts included food, together with wool and other "products of their hands," gold and silver, bread and wine. Most of the gifts were set aside by the deacons for the care of the widows, orphans, and the needy.

Enough of the bread and wine was later taken to the altar where, with the prayers of the minister (an early liturgy calls him "the president"), it was set apart to be used in the sacrament. By placing the preparation of the vessels at the Offertory, the *Service Book and Hymnal* has restored this action to a place where it aptly symbolizes the fact that God uses the things of his world (what we give him) as the vehicles of his grace (what he gives us).

With the change in thinking about the sacrament which occurred in the Middle Ages—that it was a repetition of the sacrifice of Calvary, and in its effect was equal with what our Lord did there—the mass became in its chief emphasis a thing the people gave to God instead of something he gave them.

Luther would have none of this. The Romish mass, he said, "stinketh of oblation." His scissors snipped away at the long prayer called the Canon which surrounded the Words of Institution, but his wrath was also enkindled against the prayers of the Offertory. Rather than offer a sound substitute, he cut them out. Many lament this action, arguing that he allowed a gap at the Offertory and at the Canon which might have been better handled had he suggested other suitable prayers.

As for the Offertory, it became an action with no accompaniment save the silent prayer of the minister and the singing of the congregation. One wishes that the *Service Book and Hymnal* had allowed an audible prayer here. Still there are several acceptable substitutes, and pastors who desire them may find them in books of prayer and devotion.

There is an attraction in the action taking place. As a small boy I can remember the "white tent" (as my own son labeled it) on the altar, gleaming white in the reflection of the altar candles which made communion Sundays different from other Sundays. This sense of awe has never left me. Is there a pastor who doesn't experience the same sensation when he goes silently to the altar to prepare the vessels? There is an awe and a mystery about the sacrament conveyed by those words of the hymn: "Here do I touch and handle things unseen."

If pastors feel this as do the people, how careful they must be of their actions. This is no time for play-acting and sentimental gestures. It is a time for reverent careful action.

THE PRAYER OF THE CHURCH

Here we come to a problem in our regular Sunday worship —the Prayer of the Church. Strangely enough, criticism of the prayer comes not so much from the laity as from the pastors. Some have gone so far as to omit the prescribed prayer in the book entirely and offer in its place all sorts of compositions.

A layman has nailed the issue firmly:

Instead of the beautiful and comprehensive prayer given, there is a very short *ex tempore* prayer which usually consists of a brief restatement of the main points of the sermon, asking God to give us grace to do whatever the sermon said we should do. Often there is added a brief petition for any *in the congregation* who are sick or in special trouble. And that is all.

The writer continues that there is no place in such a prayer for invoking God's blessing upon the government and its leaders, and then concludes, "There is nothing to direct our thoughts, much less our need or our desire to pray for the church universal, for missions, for the needs of the world."

The *Service Book and Hymnal* does allow for a "suitable" substitute for the Prayer of the Church, except on festivals and when there is a communion. Some will argue that because communion ought to be administered every Sunday, this rubric allows little leeway. Still the genius of our worship is not restricted here to one form of prayer. Rightly, there should be allowance for variation.

The rubric in the *Service Book and Hymnal* (p. 275) allows for variation: "The Prayer of the Church, or one of the General Prayers (p. 238) shall be used on Festivals and wherever there is a Communion. At other times the Litany or a selection from the Collects and Prayers (p. 218), or any other suitable Prayer, may be said." Still it is possible to argue that free prayer is and has been a part of the church's historic worship. One of the earliest liturgies directs that here the president shall offer prayer "as he is able."

The trouble with prayer that is not written is that it soon begins to follow a repetitious pattern and eventually becomes more tedious than a regular reading of the Prayer of the Church. Worshipers who have heard certain clergymen offer "free prayers" over a period of time can almost tell how the prayer will begin, what will be prayed for, and in exceptional cases recite word for word some of the phrases.

Free prayer, unless carefully worked out beforehand (and then is it really free?), often becomes a solemn broadcast to the Almighty of a lot of things he most certainly knows better than we. If not that, it is a rehash of the sermon, in which the pastor frequently tries again to make a point which was made in the sermon.

The keyword in the rubric is, of course, "suitable." A prayer at this point in the service ought to be comprehensive. It ought to be "for all sorts and conditions of men" and then some. It ought to be a prayer, not a lecture addressed to either God or people or both.

The Prayer of the Church is composed of thirteen paragraphs. Six of these are indented and, as provided by the rubric, may be omitted at the discretion of the pastor. Another rubric permits the pastor to make announcement in an appropriate formula when intercessions are to be included in the prayer.

I don't agree with those pastors who say that the Prayer of the Church is tedious. I once had a neighbor, a member of a Lutheran congregation, tell me she had heard our broadcast when she was forced to stay at home because of sickness. "Where did you get that lovely prayer?" she inquired. "I have never heard it before!"

One doesn't omit the Gloria in Excelsis because the same words are sung Sunday after Sunday. The prayer touches the situations of all who are present.

One way to allow for greater participation is to follow the provision of the *Service Book and Hymnal* which directs the people to say between each petition, "We beseech Thee to hear us, good Lord."

Truly the prayer is comprehensive. All areas of the Christian's life are touched by its petitions. And lest we forget those who have died in Christ, provision is made here for their remembrance. It is disappointing to some people that among Lutherans there is seldom any mention of the dead. This is probably a reaction against Roman Catholic usage which teaches that, by the prayers and offerings of the living, the state of the dead, even their salvation, can be affected. The picture of purgatory and the history of a church which exploited its people by preying upon their sympathy for their deceased loved ones, is one we don't want repeated among us.

Does that mean that we may not remember the dead? Does not the noble army of martyrs include those who have died in the twentieth century as well as the first? May I not remember with thanksgiving my own brother who gave his life for his country?

The Prayer of the Church makes allowance for remembrance, not with any thought of affecting the conditions of the departed—this we cannot do, for they are in the hands of God—but with joyful remembrance that they have returned to the Lord and Giver of life.

This prayer too is our offering. We give our gifts, and in token of their intended use, bread and wine are prepared for what follows. We give our song to put words to the silent act of placing our money upon the altar. We give our prayer, uniting the congregation we know with the church throughout the world. This then is our sacrifice, a sacrifice of thanksgiving to God.

THE FRUSTUM

Before you run for your dictionary, let me admit that you won't find "frustum" in a book on liturgics. In the *Service Book and Hymnal* after the Prayer of the Church is this rubric: "If there be no Communion, the Minister and Congregation shall say the Lord's Prayer."

In most of our congregations, the usual Sunday morning practice is to end the service here with the Benediction and a hymn. Holy Communion when it is available to the congregation is offered only at certain times, ranging from four times a year to a stated communion service on the major festivals and in each season of the church year.

In the United Lutheran Church in America, the parish norm, according to the 1958 Report on the Manifested Life of the Congregation, was 11.7 communion services a year. Five years before the norm had been 8.5. In 1953 twenty-three congregations indicated that they had a weekly communion. In 1958 the number was 41.

This practice is hardly consonant with that of the early church. Gregory Dix says a Christian in the year A.D. 300 would slip out of his house before daybreak carrying a piece of bread—a symbol of his whole life—and make his way secretly to an agreed destination. There, in a small room with ordinary people, he would offer his bread, placing it upon the table, and then with his fellow Christians, receive it and a little wine as the vehicles of God's presence.

Nor is our custom a faithful adherence to Luther's suggestions for worship. His writings and the confessions of the church bear record that the normal Sunday observance was a complete service, including sermon and sacrament. One wonders if the Reformer would recognize our services of today, particularly with the increasing emphasis given to "special" anthems and solos.

Here then is our "frustum." What was once a unit is now but a part of the whole. This is frustrating to one who likes to see things whole.

So with our chief service. To be sure, God's grace comes equally in both sermon and communion, not to mention baptism, absolution, counseling. This our confessions make quite clear. Concerning Word and sacrament, they say, "The effect of both is the same."

Still, if a worshiper who has moved through the stages of worship—confession and absolution, praise and thanksgiving, instruction and admonition, prayer and offering—is then dismissed without an opportunity to receive the assurance of God's presence in the form instituted by the Savior, isn't something wrong?

One who feels this matter keenly cannot help but know frustration. To be sure he may not wish to commune every Sunday, but shouldn't the opportunity be there?

There is something more. The Supper is a corollary of the sermon. One modern scholar has expressed the matter this way:

Penitence and the preaching of the gospel presuppose baptism and the Lord's Supper. In other words, penitence and preaching of the gospel belong only in the congregation's work through baptism and the Supper . . . Penitence and preaching therefore have no special symbol. Their symbol is always that of baptism and the Lord's Supper.

Penitence and preaching are sacramental words. They are sacramental because they announce the fulfillment of the promise. They truly give the Christ to whom the promise speaks. Therefore they are also constantly connected with the symbols which God has given in the fulfillment of the promise, i.e. the symbol of baptism and the Supper. It is only by the these symbols that penitence and preaching take place.[1]

This whole matter is under serious examination in the church today. Those who prefer to see a greater emphasis placed on the sacrament, so that there is more frequent opportunity for communion, point to the past ages of the church's history, and the careful balance that existed between sermon and sacrament. Their opponents declare that any such emphasis detracts from the importance of the sermon, tends to "cheapen" the reassurance of the Holy Communion.

[1] Regin Prenter, *Spiritus Creator* (Philadelphia: Muhlenberg, 1953), p. 151.

THE PREFACE

My wife and I once attended a wedding in an Episcopal church. As a part of the service, the bridal party received Holy Communion. Except for a few hymns and the organ music, all parts of the service were read, all, that is, with the exception of three short sentences. The bishop had prepared the vessels on the altar. Then, turning to the people, he chanted the versicles which introduce the Preface. Afterward, my wife was puzzled: "Why did that nice old man read everything, but when he got to the Preface, he began to chant?"

That's a good question and I tried to explain that the versicles are traditional but I'm afraid that my reply satisfied neither her nor myself.

Historically these versicles are quite ancient, and today almost every liturgy of Christendom uses them to introduce the second part of the service. They are a sort of stage direction spoken aloud.

As before in the Salutation preceding the Collect, the officiating minister or celebrant turns to the people and says, "The Lord be with you," and the people respond with "And with thy spirit." It is as if once again actors in the sacred drama quietly remind one another of the importance of this part of their sacred action.

But this time the "reminder" doesn't stop there. The

celebrant continues, "Lift up your hearts," and the congregation responds, "We lift them up unto the Lord." And then follows the versicle which sets the stage for what is to follow.

Remember that our Lord took up the bread and, the Scriptures continue, "when he had given thanks.. . ." This then is our invitation to imitate his actions on the night of his betrayal. This is a thanksgiving, hence the word Eucharist which is Greek for "thanksgiving." If we were to paraphrase this little threefold exchange between minister and people, it might be something like this:

℣. God be with you. This is important, pay attention.

℟. May he be with you too.

℣. Forget the things of the world and go up to the throne of God.

℟. We agree and go with you.

℣. Now let us prepare ourselves to thank him for his goodness.

℟. It's the only right thing to do.

A bit wooden perhaps, and certainly not an improvement on the form in our service book, but it helps us to understand what we sing. And if you compare "Lift up your hearts" with Lamentations 3:41 and Psalm 86:4 you catch some of the desire inherent in these ancient forms.

Having introduced the Preface with the little interchange (and it should be done from memory by the celebrant), he now turns and commences the Preface proper. There are two parts here. That which is fixed and remains unchanged from week to week is the Common Preface.

It consists of two parts, the Thanksgiving and the Ascription, and the concluding sentence which leads into the Sanctus. The variable portion, with different prayers appointed for certain days and seasons of the church year, is the Proper Preface.

Continuing in the vein begun in the last of the three versicles, the celebrant begins this prayer of thanksgiving, "It is truly meet, right, and salutary. . . ." Some of those words sound a bit archaic. Remembering that our service is a purified form of the Roman Catholic mass, one can appreciate the problem by seeing these words in Latin *"Vere dignum et justum est, aequum et salutare . . ."* Modern Roman Catholic missals translate them, "It is truly meet and just, right and availing unto salvation. . . ."

The Episcopal Book of Common Prayer, which is copied by many other Protestants, uses the words, "It is very meet, right, and our bounden duty . . . ," hardly an improvement particularly in the last words. Lutherans simply use the word "salutary," which if understood as something which is "availing to salvation" isn't bad. Again paraphrasing with a view to explaining and not improving the form, "It is truly proper, right and conducive to our salvation. . . ." In other words, we ought to be doing what we are!

A Christian's life ought to be filled with thanksgiving. One has but to remember Luther's explanation of the first article of the Creed. After making a long list of the benefits of creation, he adds, "for all of which I am in duty bound to thank, praise, serve and obey him."

But the giving of thanks is not an occasional exercise in the life of a Christian. This is not a duty to be regulated by the clock or the occasion. What would you think of a child who embraced you only when you gave him a present, but treated you with indifference the rest of the time? "We should at all times and in all places give thanks unto thee. . . ."

We do not pull God out of the closet when we need him. This is the fault with so much modern "psychological" preaching. In this preaching God is the plug that fits into the gap in our lives. Pastors afflicted with such an outlook seldom preach God as an end in himself, and the result is that when a person (however erringly) feels he has no "holes" in his life, he forgets God.

God is not simply the answer to all our problems. He is that only incidentally. God is God! And we as his creatures, both by birth and infinitely more by the new birth in baptism, owe him more than we can ever give. This is why we say, "It is truly meet, right and salutary that we should at all times and in all places give thanks" unto him.

To focus more carefully on some of the reasons for our thankfulness, there is built within the Common (or fixed) Preface a variable prayer which is called the Proper Preface (this means it is proper only to the day or the season for which it is intended).

In the *Service Book and Hymnal* there are nine such prefaces:

Advent (anticipation of the return of the Redeemer who will "make all things new").

Christmas (loving God in flesh causes us to love things unseen).

Epiphany (God's glory revealed in Christ as man).

Lent (a tree is our downfall by Adam, and is our salvation by Christ).

Easter (in which we know death is overcome).

Festival of Ascension (the hope of eternal salvation for mankind).

Festival of Pentecost (God does not leave us but sends us the Holy Ghost).

Festival of Trinity (the subject of our worship. Note: only to be used on Trinity Sunday and its octave—first Sunday after Trinity—not the whole Trinity Season).

All Saints' Day (or any time when the faithful departed are remembered) (example of the blessed dead—a pledge of our hope).

By using these Proper Prefaces, our attention is directed to the occasions commemorated in the life of our Lord and the fruits of his ministry which come from them. The fact that there now are nine ought to convince us that Holy Communion should be more than a quarterly observance. Each pinpoints the occasion for our gratitude and so helps to distribute them over the church year.

But thanksgiving, as we have said, is not a seasonal thing, and rather than end on a note which relegates our gratitude to only one time, the Preface concludes with a magnificent, all-inclusive triumphant chorus. "Therefore with Angels and Archangels, and with all the company of heaven, we laud and magnify thy glorious Name; evermore praising thee, and saying . . ."

I recall that as a Navy chaplain I frequently held communion aboard a dirty old repair ship floating about a buoy. Most of the crew was on week-end liberty. Others loafed about the ship, and a handful showed up for services. Each time the small group discouraged me. Why did there have to be so few?

Then one day I read these words: ". . . Therefore with Angels and Archangels, and with all the company of heaven. . . ." We were not a small handful. We were united with the whole body of the faithful. In churches, chapels, and cathedrals, in prisons, hospitals, rest homes, foxholes, battleships, at sickbeds, and with all the denominations and realms of heaven, our voices were united, and in that glorious unity heaven and earth sang in thanksgiving to God.

THE SANCTUS

We don't know much about angels. Children are sometimes
told that angels come from heaven to guard them in their
sleep. Theologians explain that angels are messengers of
God (that is what the word "angel" means). Scripture
speaks of hosts of angels (remember the Christmas story),
and their ranks are divided into many grades, for example
cherubim and seraphim.

It may be strange to us that our worship on a Sunday
morning extends beyond the walls of our parish church,
even beyond the limits of this world. These otherworldly
creatures join us in our praise of God. That is what we say
in our liturgy—

Therefore with Angels and Archangels and with all the company of heaven, we laud and magnify thy glorious Name; evermore praising thee. . . .

As the minister at the altar finishes these words, there is
a burst of song, and heaven and earth join in the Sanctus.

It is appropriate that the first words we sing at this point
are the words of the angels themselves. Isaiah the prophet
(6:1-3), in the year that Uzziah died, had a vision:

I saw also the Lord sitting upon a throne, high and lifted up,
and his train filled the temple. Above it stood the seraphim:
each one had six wings; with twain he covered his face, and
with twain he covered his feet, and with twain he did fly. And

one cried unto another, and said, Holy, Holy, Holy, is the Lord
of hosts: the whole earth is full of his glory.

Here are the opening words (with slight modification)
of the first part of the Sanctus (the Latin word for "holy").
One wishes that the English use of "hosts" had been retained instead of the Hebrew "Sabaoth," which may be
mistaken for "Sabbath," the day of rest.

The second part of the Sanctus brings to mind an event
in the earthly life of Christ. From the dream of Isaiah and
the majestic throne of God with its attendant echoes of
heavenly praise, we are carried back across the years to
the beginning of Holy Week. In triumph he who left the
praise of the angels to become a man, receives the praise
of men:

And the multitude that went before, and that followed, cried,
saying, Hosanna to the Son of David: Blessed is he that cometh
in the name of the Lord; Hosanna in the highest.

Like so many words in our liturgy which come from
other languages, "Hosanna" is frequently not understood.
It means "Save, I beseech Thee," and is used in the great
Hallel, a collection of Psalms 113–18 (see 118:25, 26),
which was a part of the great Jewish rituals. Some scholars
have suggested that these words were a part of the hymn
which the Lord and his disciples sang in the upper room
at the Last Supper.

The first part of the Sanctus was used frequently in
Jewish rituals. As the church began to formulate its worship there was some reluctance to use these Jewish hymns
(for fear that Christians would be regarded as a splinter
Jewish sect). By about A.D. 200 the words from Isaiah
(and one can see a close parallel in Rev. 4:8) were incorporated into the liturgy. Three hundred years later, the
second part (commonly called the *Benedictus qui venit*

from the Latin meaning "Blessed is He who comes" was added.

In the Roman mass, the words of this second section were regarded by some as an indication that with the consecration Christ would come. Hence the Roman Church directed that a bell (the so-called Sanctus bell) should be rung at the Sanctus, a practice continued to this day.

Luther in his first revision of the mass directed that the Sanctus be sung after the Words of Institution, to place the emphasis where it properly belongs, on the communion and not on the consecration. Yet Luther allowed the elevation of the bread and wine during the words "Blessed is he that cometh . . ." and there are those who feel he did this to give emphasis to the Real Presence.

In the second, or German revision, Luther substituted a paraphrase or hymn text for the Sanctus and directed that it be sung during the administration of the sacrament. Dr. Luther Reed says[1] that this was one of the least fortunate of Luther's revisions and while recounting the story of Isaiah's vision, omitted the praise of the congregation.

It is the picture formed in our minds by these words which ought to give meaning to our worship here. Someone has suggested that the scene is of Christ on the cross surrounded by the whole creation. Here before that aweful moment when God effected the salvation of mankind are gathered all that he has made. Recognizing the moment for its importance as their reconciliation, every voice is lifted to praise God for his goodness. The angels begin with the hymn of heaven, and its strains are joined to the words of men, the disciples of Christ.

Nothing before in time or space has ever come close to this moment. The enemies of God are by the cross defeated, and the whole creation with a single voice lifts its praise

[1] *The Lutheran Liturgy*, p. 332.

and adoration. In that moment we join the universe in a song of praise to God.

Our concerns, anxieties, and frustrations can in a moment be forgotten. Christ comes to this congregation, to its troubled people, to me. Oh let me sing, let me feel the joy of that moment, Hosanna in the highest!

THE CONSECRATION

Looking back across the years to that night of destiny when the disciples gathered in the upper room for the Lord's Supper, we are reminded of the simple actions of our Lord. It was a common meal, perhaps of deep ritual significance within the framework of pious Jewish practice.

The disciples, we are told, were commemorating the Passover, the aweful day when the children of Israel, protected by the promise of God, escaped the wrath of the avenging angel and so began their trek to the promised land. For us who seek to imitate that sacred moment, four features of the ritual ought to imprint themselves on our minds.

The Scriptures tell us that Christ 1) took bread, 2) gave thanks, 3) broke it, and 4) gave it to his disciples. These are the four: the use of simple elements—bread and wine—the giving of thanks, the breaking of the bread and the blessing of the cup, and the distribution.

Whatever else was added in later years, whether the simplest of prayers and hymns or the most elaborate ceremony, was of secondary importance. These four features of the institution of the Lord's Supper were paramount.

In the years that followed it was inevitable that this ritual should be repeated by those who followed Christ. He himself had given command, "This do in remembrance of me."

We know from the letters of Paul that the New Testament churches practiced this ritual. The Words of Institution in most of the Christian liturgies are taken from one of his letters (I Cor. 11:23-26), and in the preceding chapter he says: "The cup of blessing which we bless, is it not the communion of the blood of Christ? The bread which we break, is it not the body of Christ?"

But when a ritual is established it must take on form, and in a short time a pattern much like our liturgy developed in many areas of Christendom. There was a part of the service which had to do with instruction, containing hymns, lessons, and sermons. This was attended by those who were members of the church as well as those who were still being instructed, the catechumens.

The second portion was only for the initiated. Amid thanksgiving it culminated in the sacred common meal or sacrament.

At first many of the prayers were extemporaneous. Later these prayers took on definite form and in many areas are preserved to this day. Many of the prayers of the liturgy date from very early times.

Most important of the prayers of Christian worship was that which accompanied the setting apart of bread and wine. A prayer longer than others, it contained as its chief parts an offering, thanksgiving, and invocation. Usually the Words of Institution were set into this prayer as a sort of warrant for the sacred action.

The offering prayer related to the gifts which the people had brought, among them the bread and wine set upon the altar. The thanksgiving contained a remembrance of God's goodness in sending his Son and made brief reference to the chief events in the earthly life of Christ (among these, the institution as related by Paul [I Cor. 11:23-25]). The invocation was a prayer calling upon God to send the

Holy Spirit upon the people and the gifts that by his power the bread and wine might be the Body and Blood of Christ and that the people might receive the sacrament to their blessing, not their condemnation.

This generally continues to be the practice among the Eastern or Orthodox Christians and has been followed by most Protestants who have a liturgical order of service.

With the growing power of Rome and the subsequent importance of the Bishop of Rome as the head of the church, a new emphasis soon became evident in the Western or Roman Catholic Church. Instead of regarding the service primarily as a sacrament, a gift of grace, it became the custom to stress the change (and the theologians of Rome declared that it was possible to determine the precise moment) from bread to Body and wine to Blood. The liturgy came to be regarded not so much as a sacrament (God's gift to us) as a sacrifice (our gift to God), a repetition of Christ's sacrifice which had equal merit with what happened on Calvary.

The long prayer surrounding the Words of Institution was altered to convey this meaning. In the liturgy the Body and Blood of Christ are offered anew to God for the sins of the living and the repose of the dead. So said Rome, and this is evident when one studies the prayer of the Roman mass today.

Luther would have none of it. It is an abomination, he said. Returning to the earlier emphasis he took the mass in hand to make it thoroughly evangelical. And here we come to a problem. While the other Reformers had prepared new orders of service quite unlike the structure of the mass, Luther was conservative. He kept the mass, purging it of unevangelical features and setting again the gift of God as the jewel within its framework.

Only at the point of the prayer of consecration did he

seem to use a rough hand. At least so many Lutheran scholars feel. Ripping out all that followed after the Preface and the Sanctus, he permitted only the Words of Institution and the Lord's Prayer.

This practice for the most part has been followed by Lutheran churches ever since. Among the churches of Christendom, Lutherans in this use have stood alone. Moreover Luther's direction in his Latin Mass that the Words of Institution ought to precede the Lord's Prayer was contradicted by his later or German revision of the mass which directed the inverse order, a reversal which has occasioned much confusion in Lutheranism.

Luther was in revolt against the impure doctrine contained in the Roman prayer. He insisted that here, of all places, the Word of God ought to be heard, rather than the words of men.

Whatever motivated his actions, we know the results. In the more than four hundred years since the Reformation, Lutheran churches throughout the world have generally followed his direction.

In our service of Holy Communion the typically Lutheran use of the Words of Institution and the Lord's Prayer at the moment when bread and wine are set apart has given concern to many. Is it not possible, they say, to have a prayer here which carefully describes the Lutheran teaching of Holy Communion?

We believe that the Lord's Supper "is the true Body and Blood of our Lord Jesus Christ, under the bread and wine, given to us Christians to eat and to drink, as it was instituted by Christ himself." We affirm that the body and blood of Christ are present "in, with, and under" the forms of bread and wine. This presence is effected by the Word of God. Why not, then, change our liturgy to allow for a form which says just that?

Such a question has arisen in the minds of many Lutherans. When work began on the *Service Book and Hymnal*, this question confronted the representatives of the eight participating bodies. Agreeing that such a prayer, properly phrased, was not only possible but commendable, they offered a suggested form to the bodies represented.

In 1948 the matter came before the convention of the United Lutheran Church in America. The result was a rather lengthy and at times strenuous debate. Many delegates were outspoken in their criticism.

The prayer was sent back to the commission with the request that it be revised. This was an important decision. It showed that a majority was willing to accept the use of such a prayer, but wanted a revision of the suggested form. It must also be noted in addition that the new book allowed for the alternate use of the form directed by Luther in his first revision of the mass, the Words of Institution and the Lord's Prayer, in that order.

The prayer was revised and finally accepted in the form in which it appears in the *Service Book and Hymnal* (p. 11). Thus in American Lutheranism, for the first time, our congregations have an officially sanctioned Prayer of Thanksgiving in their liturgies if they desire to use it. That the need for such a prayer is being felt by other Lutherans is evidenced by the fact that in Sweden and in Germany new service books contain similar prayers.

This is the text of the prayer:

Holy art thou, Almighty and Merciful God. Holy art thou, and great is the Majesty of thy glory.

Thou didst so love the world as to give thine only-begotten Son, that whosoever believeth in him might not perish, but have everlasting life; Who, having come into the world to fulfill for us thy holy will and to accomplish all things for our salvation.

IN THE NIGHT IN WHICH HE WAS BETRAYED, [a]TOOK BREAD; AND, WHEN HE HAD GIVEN THANKS, HE BRAKE IT AND GAVE IT TO HIS DISCIPLES, SAYING, TAKE, EAT; THIS IS MY BODY WHICH IS GIVEN FOR YOU; THIS DO IN REMEMBRANCE OF ME.

AFTER THE SAME MANNER ALSO, HE [b]TOOK THE CUP, WHEN HE HAD SUPPED, AND, WHEN HE HAD GIVEN THANKS, HE GAVE IT TO THEM, SAYING, DRINK YE ALL OF IT; THIS CUP IS THE NEW TESTAMENT IN MY BLOOD, WHICH IS SHED FOR YOU, AND FOR MANY, FOR THE REMISSION OF SINS; THIS DO, AS OFT AS YE DRINK IT, IN REMEMBRANCE OF ME.

Remembering, therefore, his salutary precept, his life-giving Passion and Death, his glorious Resurrection and Ascension and the promise of his coming again, we give thanks to thee, O Lord God Almighty, not as we ought, but as we are able; and we beseech thee mercifully to accept our praise and thanksgiving, and with thy Word and Holy Spirit to bless us, thy servants, and these thine own gifts of bread and wine, so that we and all who partake thereof may be filled with heavenly benediction and grace, and, receiving the remission of sins, be sanctified in soul and body, and have our portion with all thy saints.

And unto thee, O God, Father, Son, and Holy Spirit, be all honor and glory in thy holy Church, world without end. Amen.

[a] Here he shall take the BREAD in his hand.
[b] Here he shall take the CUP in his hand.

The Words of Institution and the Lord's Prayer are a permissive alternate.

THE PAX

A pastor's ministry is obstructed by many irritants. Not the least of these is gossip. One pastor awoke one morning to find his parish in a dither over the latest of his "dictatorial changes." Back-fence rumor that morning had it: "Have you heard the latest? Now he's forbidden the bride and groom to kiss each other at the altar after the marriage ceremony!"

The pastor had recently officiated at a wedding where the newlyweds climaxed the affair with an ecstatic embrace. In Hollywood style they enfolded one another and—according to one report—their first kiss of married life lasted forty-three seconds!

After that the pastor, in counseling with prospective brides and grooms, made it a point to recommend that they save their first kiss until they were alone, or "at least be discreet."

But kissing isn't necessarily limited to lovers, and it isn't sissy stuff. Frequently Paul directed the people to whom he wrote to "greet one another with an holy kiss," and so did Peter. Whether this was simply a cheek-to-cheek embrace, as is still the oriental custom, isn't of great importance. It was a simple gesture conveying a feeling of affection.

No doubt it was from this apostolic advice that the "kiss

of peace" became a greeting among Christians in their as-
semblies. Later the symbolic gesture became a part of
Christian worship, and was attached to a blessing given to
the people before they communed. Originally, this blessing
had been more elaborate. But eventually it was shortened
to the form in which we have it today, "The peace of the
Lord be with you alway."

As so frequently happened with gestures assimilated
into the liturgy, the kiss soon became strictly a ceremonial
feature. The celebrating minister "embraced" the deacon,
who in turn passed on the embrace to the others in the
sanctuary, but it seldom went further than that.

In time a pax-board or *osculatorium* was used. This was
a small metal or wooden piece marked with religious symbols, which at the proper place in the liturgy was kissed by
the celebrant. He in turn gave it to the deacon who also
kissed it and passed it on. Contact with the people in
their worship had been lost, and the result was a meaningless ceremonial that has for the most part disappeared.

Luther found great satisfaction with the Pax (although
no mention is made of the ceremonial kiss), and directed
that it be used as a blessing of the gospel announcing the
forgiveness of sins, "the only and most worthy preparation
for the Lord's table . . . hence I wish it announced with
face toward the people as the bishops were accustomed
to do."

This is the more significant feature of the Pax and we
do well to appreciate its significance for us at this point in
the service. But what of the kiss of peace? Apart from a
few rather obscure instances in some of the Orthodox
churches and in certain of the ceremonial directions of the
Roman Church it is almost universally ignored. Practical
considerations make its return almost impossible.

But there have been serious efforts to return to the

gesture in somewhat modified form and so incorporate it into modern liturgies. In the Church of South India "the kiss of peace" is observed as a part of its newly created liturgy. At the proper time the officiating minister takes the right hand of the assisting minister in his own and covers it with his left hand, as does the assistant. Along with this physical contact, he speaks the words: "The peace of the Lord" or "The Peace of God be with you."

The assistant then conveys the "kiss" to others in the sanctuary, who then carry it to the people where it is exchanged down through the nave until all present have "saluted one another with an holy kiss."

The gesture isn't of the utmost importance and the "parish boss" who piously grasps the hand of his neighbor may have little if any real concern, let alone love, for the person to whom he has conveyed the peace of God. Looking back upon the events of the night in Gethsemane we may remember that the gesture of a kiss, usually an act of affection, became a sign of betrayal.

Signs or symbols, to have any real meaning, are outward expressions of the innermost thoughts of our minds and hearts. Without this foundation within, all of the most solemn gestures, actions, or ceremonies are no more than sham.

Luther rightly seizes upon the very heart of the Pax. We would come to the altar to receive God's gift of himself. We would clear out the debris of our daily lives—disturbances, frustrations, hatred, envy, and discontent—which plague us all. We would offer God a dwelling place for his Spirit.

Our Lord had strong words of advice for such a moment. "Therefore if thou bring thy gift to the altar, and there rememberest that thy brother hath ought against thee; leave there thy gift before the altar, and go thy way; first be reconciled to thy brother, and then come and offer thy gift."

One Christian liturgy exhorts communicants to confess their sins in this fashion: "Ye who do truly and earnestly repent you of your sins, and are in love and charity with your neighbors. . . ."

We can't expect that God will dwell in a house where bad feelings for another of his creatures remain with us. The Scriptures say that a man who loves God and yet hates his brother is a liar. We may try to hedge and say that we don't really hate another. But when there is bad feeling, can we honestly say that we love? And if we cannot say that we love our brother, dare we say that we love God?

Who hasn't known that moment when after months and sometimes years of bitterness, backbiting, and malicious slander, one is suddenly confronted with his enemy? In a moment, a rare impulse (ought we not rather say, the work of the Holy Spirit) makes you thrust out your hand in friendship, and in the same spirit he grasps yours. How utterly ridiculous the long days of rancor now appear, and how blessed the reconciliation!

So we would have God come in to dwell with us. We approach the moment that is a rendezvous with love. As the minister turns from the altar and lifts his voice in blessing, the blessing of peace, we know that God's Spirit has made us ready and we bid him enter.

AGNUS DEI

The Day Christ Died, by Jim Bishop, describes the events which led to the crucifixion. One scene depicts the temple ritual of sacrifice. Amid the ceremony of chanted psalms, vestments, and incense, a lamb is slain. The description denoted the symbolism which dramatized for the Jews of that day their need for a Savior.

Against this symbolical drama, the writer begins the narrative of those moments which lead up to and include the perfect sacrifice of Jesus Christ. First there is the observance of the Passover. A lamb is slain. In the family ritual the deliverance from Egypt is represented and the hoped-for delivery from bondage is sought anew.

Then, in those aweful moments which follow, the sacrifice is accomplished on the cross. The parallel is perfect. As a lamb symbolized the offering which one day would have to be made, so the Lamb is offered.

For centuries the lamb had been a symbol in Judaism. The prophet Isaiah (53:7) pictures the Messiah "brought as a lamb to the slaughter."

John the Baptist, one day as he beheld Jesus coming through the crowd, cried, "Behold the Lamb of God, which taketh away the sin of the world."

No doubt those words from Isaiah rang through the mind of Christ as he prepared to celebrate the Passover with his disciples. Certainly he must have hoped that the parallel which was to be accomplished on the first Good Friday would bear its imprints upon their minds. Paul certainly caught it, for in his first letter to the Corinthians (5:7) he says, "Christ our passover is sacrificed for us," words which have found their place in the Introit for Easter.

It isn't difficult to see how the symbolism was carried over into Christian worship. Such attempts to put into sign language the great truths of the faith became a part of Christian worship from an early day. When the Lord's Supper was celebrated, the breaking of a loaf of bread was identified with the sacrifice of Christ upon the cross.

In the Eastern churches a hymn using the words of John the Baptist was composed for use in the service at just about the point it occurs today. Pope Sergius I, who was from the East, decreed in the year 700 that the hymn be used in all of the liturgies of the church. This hymn is almost the same as the one we use today, except that the words, "O Christ," have been added to the beginning of each line, making it a prayer.

At the time of the Reformation it was almost universally retained in Lutheran worship, and in some places the rubric directed that the communion begin with the singing of the Agnus Dei (AHN-yoos DAY-ee).

There is something most appropriate about the use of the Agnus Dei at this point. Having been instructed in God's Word through the lessons and the sermon, we have made our offerings in response to that Word, and now fulfil the command of the Savior to "do this. . . ." Bread and wine have been set upon the altar. The pastor, in the place of Christ, repeats the sacred actions of that night of betrayal. In a very real sense we Christians celebrate the new Passover with our Lord. Having imitated the actions of the first Supper and prayed for God's gracious blessing we are assured of God's peace. Then we pray in song to Christ.

Evangelical Christianity is careful to avoid the error of
· Rome which would make of each mass an action equivalent to the action on the cross. No sacrifice we make to
God can gain our salvation for us. The only sacrifice we
can ever make to God is an offering of thanksgiving for
what he has already given us. In our worship we offer him
our praise, our gifts, and ourselves.

There is a sense in which the Sacrament of the Altar is
a sacrifice. Christ's death, and the benefits derived from it,
are made real to us in this liturgical action. True, it is a
memorial. He commanded us to do it "in remembrance
of me."

But is this action only a picture of something that happened two thousand years ago? If that's so, we might just
as well hang a large painting of the Last Supper in our
churches so that people can see it any time they want to
and so eliminate all of the fuss and bother of long services.

What Christ accomplished on Calvary effected the salvation of all men for all time. Only a few of the people
affected by his action were present at the precise moment
when their salvation was accomplished. The forgiveness of
our sins is conditioned upon what he did on the cross.

How bridge the gaps of time and space? To use one
figure of speech, it was all paid for then, but our sins are
in the present, not in the past. Hence the service of the
Lord's Supper brings into the present the sacrifice on
Calvary and so men are assured that by Christ's perfect
obedience "even unto death" they are forgiven.

Such a view gains credence in the light of the words of
the Agnus Dei. Notice that the words are "that takest away
the sins of the world," not "who has taken. . . ." Although
we are in time and space removed from Calvary by thousands of years our sins of this day are still removed by
Christ.

So we sing this ancient hymn. A modern scholar has reminded us that we must never think we have understood any teaching of Luther unless we have reduced it to his central doctrine of the forgiveness of sins. For Luther this was not simply a negative thing, but with the emptying of all our faults and the guilt and punishment attached, there comes, as he says in the Catechism, "life and salvation."

This then is our prayer in the Agnus Dei. Mindful of the Savior who comes down upon our altar and gives us himself, veiled in the forms of bread and wine, who by his death accomplished our forgiveness, we pray that he may come to us and in coming bring us his peace.

THE COMMUNION

Billy Graham, with all of the techniques of modern advertising, invaded New York. From gigantic billboards the face of this clean-cut, latter-day John the Baptist looked down upon the hurrying throngs. His name in brilliant red letters was emblazoned on posters, signposts, and great banners.

"My only specialty," he said, "is soul-winning." No doubt under the skillful, appealing direction of his preaching, many people in Madison Square Garden went forth to make their "decision for Christ."

What happens to those people after the crusade? Suppose that after the last echo of an old gospel song drifts off into the rafters of the Garden, Billy Graham had exceeded the records of Billy Sunday in 1917 and brought more than a hundred thousand souls to the moment of decision. What then? What happens to John Doe or Mary Smith who in the atmosphere of fervent preaching, gospel songs, and the enthusiasm of those about them also went forward to "decide for Christ"? Can they, for the rest of their lives, look back to the moment of their "conversion" and from that moment receive the stimulation to face the dull, dreary, and many times anxious moments which will confront them? Memories are not enough. Strength comes from repeated encounters with joy.

Certainly Billy Graham, were he asked, would admit this. He has told us that his own spiritual strength is fed by constant communion with God. He prays frequently. He pores over the Scripture zealously. Any Christian who has dedicated himself to Christ does it too.

But is that all? Are these the only means that the Spirit uses to feed us with the bread of heaven for our growth in grace?

We know that in addition to the sustenance of the Spirit which comes through preaching, reading of the Scriptures, absolution, and the mutual conversation of the things of God, there are also the sacraments. God in his wisdom has provided the common ordinary things of the world in such a way that by using them as he has commanded, we know he comes to us.

What is water but the most common of our earthly materials? Yet when we use water with his Word, as he bade us, we know that a man, a woman, even a tiny infant experiences a new birth.

But God doesn't stop with our baptism, as if it were all that he does to fortify us. Baptism is a birth, a new birth as a child not of this world but of eternity. It is an entrance into life, and of course life has to be sustained or it will die.

The new life which comes out of the water of baptism needs the food of the spirit. Among the means by which God sustains that life is the Sacrament of the Altar.

There are some people who say that what we need is more and better preaching and less ritual. We do need preaching which is urgent, which lifts us out of our complacency and makes us think.

But preaching is not the only means. Perhaps the reason that more of our people in recent years have come to take greater comfort in Holy Communion is that worshipers in our churches have found a certainty, a positive and sure blessing, in the sacramental meal which is not always available to them in some preaching.

Sermons may be subjective, full of clichés, rambling, condemnatory, collections of pious little stories without any relevance to the life of the hearer. The sacrament, set in the framework of formulas which are quite clear, promises what Christ gave, and gives what he promised.

Luther said: "When I preach of his [Christ's] death, this is a public sermon in the congregation in which I mention nobody in particular; whoever takes it to heart, takes it to heart. But when I give it specifically to the one who receives it . . . this is something more than the general sermon. For although precisely the same thing that is present in preaching is also present in the sacrament and vice versa, nevertheless there is this advantage that here a specific person is meant. In a sermon no individual is indicated or portrayed, but in the sacrament that which the sermon conveys is given to you and to me in particular." [1]

So we come to that altar. This is more than a fellowship meal which looks back in fond memory to the night of the first of many such suppers. Hence Lutherans do not remain in their seats and have the food brought to them. The emphasis in our method of receiving Holy Communion, on the other hand, has been to combine the communal meal with the individual communion of the believer with the Lord. That is why we leave our places and go to the altar.

Once there, it has been the tradition of Lutheranism for the most part to kneel for the communion. Originally the people stood to receive the sacrament. This is still the custom in Orthodox churches. From about the twelfth century it became the practice to kneel.

The Reformers continued this custom but the practice of standing reappeared, particularly in those sections where

---

[1] Erlangen Edition of Luther's Works, 29, p. 345.

the bread and wine were not thought to be the vehicles of
the Body and Blood, but only signs. Unfortunately this
gave rise to strife in the church and one was soon identified
in his beliefs about the Real Presence on the basis of his
posture, Lutherans kneeling, Reformed people standing.

The Lutheran Church has never laid down a rule about
which is proper although there are those who say that
kneeling more fittingly expresses the right spirit of the
moment, born of reverence and humility. Yet sometimes
practical considerations favor standing.

There is no excuse for sloppiness in the church or any-
where else. You can get a good idea of a person's attitude
toward life by observing the way in which he uses the things
of life—food, clothing, possessions. Sloppiness in the use
of things is usually the outer sign of a careless and indiffer-
ent attitude toward life itself.

It is in the Holy Communion that I have seen examples
of sloppiness which make me feel that the persons responsible have no interest in what they are doing. In hope that
conditions will improve, I offer some suggestions regarding
good taste in the celebration of the sacrament.

There was a time in the Lutheran Church when everyone
received the wine from one cup. No one thought much
about it. Then, about the beginning of this century, everyone became concerned about hygiene. As a result individual communion glasses were introduced in some of our
parishes.

In 1917 the Ministerium of Pennsylvania, having asked
for an opinion from the Philadelphia Seminary faculty, accepted the report which said that the kind of container used
in administering the sacrament is not an essential. The
report added that "in the administration of the sacrament,
the communicant should receive the wine, at the altar,
poured by the minister, from a common cup into the indi-

vidual receptacle held by the communicant."

The synod's resolution provided that this method should be employed in case "a congregation formally decides to abandon the historical method of administration."

In recent years some churches have adopted the use of a group of trays loaded with little glasses already filled with wine in the sacristy. These are stacked in the middle of the altar. Certainly the 1917 ruling of the Ministerium is the only satisfactory solution if people are repulsed by the common cup. This method at least recognizes the symbolism behind the one cup which is stressed by both our Lord and St. Paul.

I feel that the common cup perpetuates and strengthens the symbolism mentioned in the Holy Scriptures. If the congregation adopts the use of the individual glasses, then the wine should be poured from a chalice into the glass of each communicant. This chalice should be fitted with a small pouring lip so that the administration can be done easily. If a congregation already owns a set of trays, these can still be used for the distribution of the glasses as the communicants come forward to the altar. But I feel that the wine should not be poured into the glasses until the administration to each communicant.

As for the communicants, here are some practical suggestions. Women going to the altar should remember to blot their lipstick before leaving the pew. Purificators, not to mention pastors' fingers, can get awfully messy with the thick red stuff. And no large picture hats, please! Some women don't realize how difficult it is to see a woman's mouth or hands if she is wearing a large cartwheel and her head is bowed.

Go to the place assigned you and kneel reverently. Lift your face when you are about to receive either element. It makes it easier for the pastor. It seems almost sacrilegious to tell communicants that their mouths should be empty as they come to the altar.

If you receive from the chalice, let the minister touch it to your lips and then you guide the flow of wine by pushing lightly against the base of the chalice.

If you use the little glass, accept it from the usher and carry it in front of you as you go to the altar in *both* hands, not closing your fist around it and dangling your arm at your side.

When you have taken your place at the rail, hold the glass between your thumb and forefinger of your right hand, and rest your right hand upon your left. Thus if the minister moves from left to right he is in a good position to serve you.

Drink all of the contents of the glass. Don't drink only a part and then dangle the glass so that the wine spills out upon the floor. When you are dismissed, carry your glass to the place where it is to be surrendered, and set it down carefully. Don't do what a friend told me he had seen done in one of our churches. The communicants upon dismissal filed past a stand placing their glasses *upside down* on a wooden tray. You can imagine the result. Above all, whatever you do, do it reverently.

These practical matters are important, but it is the words which convey the real meaning; "The Body of Christ, given for thee," "The Blood of Christ, shed for thee."

This then is our communion, the high point of the service. All that has been done before has led us to the moment when in a very real sense Jesus Christ enters into our hearts.

Just as he walked the earth once before, although in a different form, now just as truly he walks the earth to dwell within us. Purged of our sins, cleared of our doubts, we come before the altar to receive him. And, wonder of wonders, according to his promise, he comes to us.

THE NUNC DIMITTIS

Forerunner of the liturgy in the *Service Book and Hymnal* was the Common Service of 1888. The men who prepared it—Edward Traill Horn, Beale M. Schmucker, and G. U. Wenner—had to establish some rule to guide them in preparing a service for American Lutherans. They wanted to be sure they had investigated the best of all Christian worship before they compiled their new service.

They established this standard: "The common consent of the pure Lutheran liturgies of the sixteenth century, and where there is not an entire agreement among them, the consent of the largest number of those of greatest weight." They based their work upon the Lutheran liturgies of the Reformation and immediate post-Reformation period. There were many of these. From them the compilers of the Common Service tried to establish a general pattern. Where there were differences, they were guided by the majority of those liturgies which had exerted the greatest influence on the church.

But in one outstanding instance they ignored the rule. This violation occurred with the use of the Nunc Dimittis in the Communion Service.

The words Nunc Dimittis are the first words of the Latin translation of Simeon's hymn in the Gospel of Luke (2: 22-32). Mary and Joseph, being pious Jews, obeyed the

126

ceremonial law of Moses faithfully. After the prescribed period following the delivery of the infant, Mary was required by Jewish law to go to the temple and make a sacrificial offering of a pair of turtledoves or two young pigeons.

It was while observing this ritual in the temple at Jerusalem that Mary and Joseph with their baby were met by an old man, Simeon. He saw the couple and their child. Taking the infant in his arms he sang a hymn of thanksgiving:

Lord, now lettest thou thy servant depart in peace, according to thy word: For mine eyes have seen thy salvation, Which thou hast prepared before the face of all people; A light to lighten the Gentiles, and the glory of thy people Israel. (Luke 2:29-32)

This is the Nunc Dimittis.

Along with the Nunc Dimittis there are two other selections taken from the New Testament which became established hymns in the worship of the early church: the Magnificat (Luke 1:46-55), sung by the Virgin Mary upon her visitation to her cousin Elizabeth to tell her the news the angel had given her, and the Benedictus (Luke 1:68-79), a thanksgiving by Zacharias, the father of John the Baptist. (Like the Nunc Dimittis, both hymns are named from their first words in Latin.)

These hymns were valued by Christians for their beauty and meaning. In time, particularly with the development of the monastic system of specified hours of prayer throughout the day, these hymns became identified with the church's daily prayer program. The Benedictus alternated with the Te Deum at Matins in the morning. The Magnificat was sung at Vespers, and at the last prayer hour of the day, or Compline, the Nunc Dimittis was used. Simeon's hymn of dismissal fitted into the late evening hour of prayer.

With the reduction of the monastic hours of prayer to two—Matins and Vespers—in Lutheranism, the Benedictus was retained for the morning and the Magnificat and the Nunc Dimittis included in Vespers.

But the Lutheran service of Holy Communion makes an almost unique use of the Nunc Dimittis. Some of the ancient Greek liturgies used this canticle in the liturgy at its end, but neither the Roman Catholic nor the Anglican orders followed the practice. Luther used it in neither of his two revisions of the mass, but it is found in the early Swedish liturgy and in at least two of the early German liturgies.

The rubric in the *Service Book and Hymnal* regarding its use after communion is permissive. This means that the Nunc Dimittis may be used at this place. It is hard to think of anything else that would be a satisfactory substitute. The Scriptures (Matt. 26:30) say concerning the close of the Last Supper, "And when they had sung a hymn, they went out into the mount of Olives."

So we too, following our Lord's Supper, sing a hymn. As to the aged Simeon, so to us the Christ has come. Not in any symbolical fashion, as if we only remembered this tiny Babe, but in a real incarnate sense. Christ comes to us under the forms of bread and wine. For a moment time stands still and the incarnate God comes to us. How joyously we can sing,

". . . for mine eyes have seen thy salvation:

which thou hast prepared before the face of all people."

THE POST-COMMUNION VERSICLE
AND COLLECT

What pastor hasn't thrilled to a church full of people on a "communion Sunday"? His joy has turned to sorrow however when, in turning from the altar after covering the sacred vessels, he beholds some empty seats. Some people can't sit still. They receive God's precious gift and then head for a side door.

One pastor, noticing that certain members always chose their places on communion Sundays so as to be in the first table and leave early, instructed the ushers to reverse the usual procedure—"so the last would be first, and the first last."

Certainly no one would think of accepting a gift without thanking the donor. It is terribly bad manners. Yet every time the most precious gift of all is given, a few recipients take it and never bother to express thanks.

We need to give thanks. It is the only response we can properly give to God. To say thanks is to render the homage due him and him alone. That is why from very early times the liturgy was called the Eucharist, the giving of thanks that Christians coming to worship God received of him more than comfort, strength, or answer to prayer. God's gift was not a memento of himself, something to cheer them through evil days. God's gift then, as it is now, is himself. And in joyous response, filled with the grace of his presence, his people give thanks.

Thus everything that follows a person's reception of holy communion is a thanksgiving. The entire service from that point is called the Post-Communion. A communicant returning to his place from the altar has ample time to offer the quiet private prayers of gratitude that ought to follow on this moment.

Then, as the vessels are covered and the congregation rises, all sing the hymn Nunc Dimittis. This is each person's hymn of praise. With my fellow members of the Body of Christ *I* stand before the God who now dwells within me and I sing *my* thanks.

But the assembled congregation is never a collection of individuals. We are the Body of Christ, the parts of a whole, and individualism dissolves into unity. The minister, facing the altar, speaks the words so frequently found in the Psalms (note the opening verses of Psalms 105, 106, 107, 118, 136) and the worshipers respond in the traditional antiphon, Psalm 105. Here is the invitation to unite in thanksgiving and the reason why we ought to respond in thanks.

Then follows the Post-Communion thanksgiving collect (the first of four).

We may be most happy with the change made here in the traditional order of the mass. Instead of an abrupt dismissal, *Ite missa est,* which means literally, "Go, it is over," there is a feature which is traditionally Lutheran. It would be more accurate to say, "traditionally Luther's." The prayer is his composition. Although drawn from various pre-Reformation sources it reflects the Reformer's desire to express at this place in the service the thanks one ought to feel. Thus in almost every Lutheran liturgy this classic prayer of Luther has found its place as a part of the Post-Communion.

Notice the pattern of the prayer.

The first thought is of thanksgiving. This is our duty and gratefully we perform it. Sometimes the words, "Thank you," seem shallow. A gift has overwhelmed us. Not always is it an extravagant donation of wealth. It may be the caress of a tiny child, a hand-picked bouquet of flowers, an amateurish attempt at handcraft, or an heirloom of sentimental value. But we recognized that the giver intended to give himself. Our feeble "thank you" seems small return for the gift.

So with God. What is adequate return for his gift of himself? Can we really do anything? Yet we know we ought.

Then too we acknowledge that the sacrament is a gift. We will not pervert the testament of the upper room and make of it our gift to God. He comes to us in it.

It is true that there is a sacrificial element in the service, but chiefly the liturgy achieves its desired and intended purpose when it is recognized as the gift of God. Against the modern secular feeling that one gets what he pays for, God gives us himself. Luther recognized this truth and set it into the prayer.

We must be careful however to accept this gift worthily. Not everyone who receives the Body and Blood of Christ in the sacrament does so to his salvation. Some, as Paul says, eat and drink to their condemnation.

A Christian must be careful not to judge others, only himself. So he unites with his fellows in this prayer: "And we beseech thee, of thy mercy, to strengthen us through the same in faith toward thee and in fervent love toward one another."

How often has a pastor been met with "But Pastor, I

don't feel worthy to go to communion. I'm not good enough!"

Not good enough! Who is? And how better find comfort and strengthening faith, the answer to doubts, and the determination to live in love toward all men than in allowing God to dwell in us. And that is what the sacrament is—God dwelling in us. We are new creatures. God in his Word—through baptism, preaching, confession and absolution, holy communion, and other means, comes to us to find a home. If we but let him enter, our life is renewed.

That is why one must never think of worship as only that which takes place in the church on Sunday. Worship begins there, at font and altar. From pulpit and lectern there comes flowing to us the blessed grace of God. We then, filled with his Presence, go forth into the world with faith and love. We bear in our conversation the marks of our assurance in God's love in Christ. This is our trust. Others seeing it in us cannot escape its power.

THE BENEDICAMUS AND THE
BENEDICTION

How does one say goodby? Parting from loved ones is often difficult. Who doesn't remember the heart-rending scenes in railroad stations and at docksides during the war? The best way to say farewell is to say it quickly.

That's what happens in the liturgy. There ought to be no long-drawn-out conclusions. That's why it is a mistake to make too much of choir recessionals, the posturing of acolytes, and "chime-bonging" organ postludes.

We've been in the presence of God. We have made our offering. He has given us his wondrous gift. There's only one thing to do: say "thank you" and leave.

So for the last time in the service, we exchange a little word of admonition to one another. We are about to go home. The minister says to the people, now fed by the Bread of heaven, "The Lord be with you." They respond, "And with thy spirit." Take God with you into your homes, shops, offices and stores. Keep him in your thoughts, deeds, and words.

The Benedicamus, which is a Latin word meaning, "we bless," is the name we give to the versicle and response which follow. It is the doxology one finds frequently in the Psalms, and to it is added a word which characterizes the whole liturgy as the Eucharist, the giving of thanks.

That's the way the church used to worship. It was felt that to add elaborate endings after the people had communed was to detract from the grandeur of the gift. In the early days of Christianity, communicants were dismissed with a simple word, "Depart in peace."

In the eleventh century, a benediction was added. The form was something like this: "May God Almighty, the Father, the Son, and the Holy Ghost, bless you." By the time of the Reformation this benediction had become quite elaborate.

With Luther's revision of the mass, a form was introduced which has since come to be regarded as peculiarly Lutheran. This form is from Numbers 6:22-27.

And the Lord spake unto Moses, saying, Speak unto Aaron and unto his sons, saying, On this wise ye shall bless the children of Israel, saying unto them,

The Lord bless thee, and keep thee:

The Lord make his face shine upon thee, and be gracious unto thee:

The Lord lift up his countenance upon thee, and give thee peace.

And they shall put my name upon the children of Israel; and I will bless them.

Some have felt it strange that in concluding a service so marked by the New Testament, a blessing from the Old Testament should be used. Much better, they say, would be the use of one of the blessings from Paul's letters, as we do in Matins and Vespers. Against opinions like these it must be borne in mind that the Aaronic benediction (so named because it was given by God to be used by Aaron and his sons) is the only benediction commanded by God.

It is the office of the pastor to speak this age-old blessing. Particularly in Lutheran circles, it has been the custom to permit only the pastor to give it or, for that matter, any benediction. When used by lay-people in their meetings, the custom has been to change the pronoun from "thee" to "you" or "us," thus making the traditional blessing into a prayer.

Luther, who had suggested the Aaronic benediction as a form of blessing in his Latin revision of the mass, later made it the only form in the German revision of 1526. "I believe," he said, "Christ used something of this kind when he blessed his disciples as he ascended into heaven."

Thus the last word of the service is strongly sacramental, God giving us something. This is not a prayer, and the pastor ought not try to improve the liturgy by adding the word "may" before the Benediction. This is a blessing from God. It is not conditional. People ought to expect to receive God's blessing as they go forth from the church.

From Dr. Luther Reed[1] we get an appreciation of the word which concludes the Benediction: "peace." "No finer or more spiritual word in the vocabulary of devotion could be found with which to conclude the Service than the word 'peace.' We begin our worship by confessing our sin. . . . We conclude with the assurance of forgiveness and peace. Upon this note, which has been sounded again and again in the Pax, the Agnus Dei, and the Nunc Dimittis, the entire service of thanksgiving and communion comes to rest."

The addition to this traditional blessing deserves notice. In the Church of Sweden it was the custom to add the words, "In the Name of the Father, and of the Son, and of the Holy Ghost," following the Benediction. Unlike its use at the beginning of the service, this formula is not now an invocation but a sacramental blessing.

Thus this phrase is used by us in the marriage service blessing, the formula of absolution, the order for ordination, and in the dedication of a house. Muhlenberg, in pre-

[1] *The Lutheran Liturgy*, p. 385.

paring the first liturgy for the Lutheran Church in North America, added the phrase to the Aaronic benediction, a practice followed by the *Service Book and Hymnal.*

In giving the Benediction the pastor stands at the altar facing the people with uplifted arms. Some have suggested that the use of both arms is appropriate to the Aaronic blessing and symbolically suggests the extended arms of Christ upon the cross.

As the minister turns to the altar for his final devotions, the congregation responds, Amen. Although the *Service Book and Hymnal* indicates a single Amen, there is nothing wrong with the threefold or sevenfold forms, provided that this is a congregational response. Intricate and operatic settings which might be fine for choirs but difficult for the congregation are not to be used.

EPILOGUE

The Benediction has been given and the candles snuffed. The last echo of the organ fades and the people leave the church. From the house of God they go to their homes.

What is the effect of this Sunday ritual, repeated in churches across the land? Do these men and women and children go to their daily lives invigorated by a sense of God, or has it all been part of the pattern of ordinary existence?

To a Christian, going to church is supposed to mean something. Set apart from other men because he has declared his acceptance of Christ's call, a Christian is different. He knows that his spiritual life, just like his body, must be fed.

To be a Christian, a man is not simply to get his ticket and then go his merry way until the time of departure. Baptism and confirmation are but the beginning. From that time until he leaves this world, a Christian must return frequently to the fountain of God's grace, there to find the strength required to sustain him in his pilgrimage of faith.

The Christian believes that God speaks to him in such moments. As plainly as he hears the words of men, and with even greater clarity at times, the Christian hears God's words.

His first encounter with this word has something like the

effect of Pentecost on the disciples of Christ. It is as if
God's Word ignites a fire within a man's heart. God's Word
gives him understanding, purpose, and peace. He is a
new man.

But the Christian cannot live on the strength of that
moment alone. The flame enkindled by God's Word may
fade. Other interests, enthusiasms, desires may tend to
draw him from the dying embers into the darkness from
which he once emerged. Something must be done to fan
those coals into a flame.

That is why the Christian goes to church. He knows that
God's Word calls him back and that, in the place set apart
for worship, among his fellows whose demands are like his
own, he will find the fire. So the Christian joins his fellows
on Sundays and holy days, not out of any sense of duty
but because he knows he must have what the church offers.
He is not perfect, and is conscious of his error and ready
to admit it. He hears again the voice of God and in praise
he expresses his thanksgiving for that voice which sets his
soul afire.

He gives his offering in gratitude although he knows
that it is nothing. And God whose love is borne on the
flames of heavenly fire comes to dwell with man. In the
church God gives man the greatest gift—himelf.

This is what we mean by liturgy. It is all that a Christian
does both inside and outside the church. It is that dramatic
interchange in love between creature and Creator. It is
the act of mutual love. In short, liturgy is service of God.

If from this sacred action so much can come, isn't it
necessary that one understand and fully appreciate what
he does in church? Dare those who are called Christians
ever allow themselves to become a congregation of hypo-
crites, paying service with their lips, yet allowing their
hearts and minds to be untouched?

We must be alert to what is required of us. Much attention has been given in times past to this or that phase of the church's life. We pride ourselves on firm adherence to the true faith. We demand thorough training before one can be permitted to come to the altar. We are encouraged to seek out others in great evangelism programs and practice faithfully the kind of stewardship which enables the church to do greater things. All these are right and good, but we must never forget that our first response is to worship God.

All of life is an act of worship. Some Christians show more tender concern in a simple act of love than many churchgoers show in much chanting and prayers. But this is not to condemn the moment from which our strength and devotion flow.

"There is too much emphasis on liturgy," some protest. "Why can't we do things simply?" True liturgy is like eating. It is essential. It is the time-honored pattern or order of our worship. It represents the efforts of years of Christian devotion to find the forms which best express the mind of man as he bows before his God.

To be sure, these forms may become mere words, but is that condition the fault of the man or the form? It is strange that when man forsakes these forms in search of something freer or more fervent, he soon finds himself creating a new liturgy. The church's history has been marked by such moments.

Prayers have to come from the heart, not a book. Hymns must have less of the dust of centuries and more of the pull on the heartstrings. Yet free prayers and fervent gospel songs can soon run their course and eventually, a fixed pattern develops.

It is not enough simply to use the forms Sunday after Sunday. We must think them through. What do the words mean? What is expected of me? What is God saying to me?

But we must not stop with our study. The churchg
must make the forms his from his heart. Words from
book become words from our hearts. Words from a pul
are words spoken to us. And bread and wine are the fo
of heaven given for us.

This then is our liturgy, a constantly burning flame
fore the altar of God which keeps alive within us the fla
which God enkindled there. Day by day we are awaken
pricked by the Spirit, and day by day in our liturgy
blaze anew.

Type used in this book
Body, 11 on 13 and 10 on 11 Times Roman
Display, Caledonia
Paper: White Standard Antique "R'